ZERO

'Sue Ja Joo's plays are a vivid portrait of life burdened by the loss of destiny through an array of characters trapped on a stage without exit.'

—Ko Hyeong-ryeol
Poet

'Joo masterfully arranges elements of time and space in a unique fashion, seamlessly creating a link to reality. Within her lawlessly-free dramatic form, Joo gently poses the question on how we, the reader or audience, should define reality.'

—Kim Kwang-Lim
Director & Playwright

'If your soul is still seeking freedom, you are ready to enter the world of Zero.'

—Oh Hyun-sung
The Today Newspaper

Also by
SUE JA JOO

Fiction

Snowstorm in Buffalo (2003)

A Red Chair (2009)

The Garden of Fog (2012)

Night Picture of Rain Sound (2017)

The Search for the Novel Haerye (2024)

Poetry

Riding on a Butterfly's Back (2009)

The Landscape Through Translucent Glass (2011)

Others

Borges Invenciones (2014)

Aha! and Eh? A Marriage of the Sciences and Humanities (2020)

The Cloudburst and the Downpour (2021)

Collections of Classic Mini-Fiction (2021)

ZERO

FOUR MODERN PLAYS BY

SUE JA JOO

Translated from Korean
by Jennifer M. Cho

PAGE ADDIE PRESS
UNITED KINGDOM

ZERO

Author: Sue Ja Joo

Translated by Jennifer M. Cho
Edited by Susan Blanshard

A catalogue record of this book is available from the British Library
ISBN 978-1-916709-97-3

Cover design by Bruce Blanshard

Published by
Page Addie Press, United Kingdom

CONTENTS

To my grandson
Benjamin Lucas Kwon Oh

FORWARD

Exploring the Theatrical World of Sue Ja Joo

Kim Kwang-Lim
Director & Playwright

All artistic endeavors, including literature, are derivative of reality. This is because human thought (i.e. language) originates from the real world. Plays, which are written to be performed on stage, are particularly more intertwined with our reality. Bound within the physical limitations of a single stage, live actors communicate with a breathing audience – this demands a stronger emphasis on realism than any other form of art.

However, according to Aristotle's concept of mimesis, art does not cease as a mere imitation of an imperfect reality; it is to be seen as a natural human capacity and a valuable tool for understanding and experiencing the internal and external complexities of life. In other words, it must present some form of metaphysical value that transcends reality. Thus, the key to fully understanding a piece, along with the worldview of its author, comes from examining how a play relates to or departs from factual realism, and how the playwright approaches and produces that stance.

From this perspective, the plays of Sue Ja Joo stand out. Her views and expressions of reality are varied and complex. Not only does she suggest that our world consists of infinite realities over the one we see; they are also tightly woven together, to continuously influence and infiltrate without boundaries. While most of us choose to live and believe a singular truth, Joo introduces a fresh world where other realities intervene and participate.

Perhaps this is why she makes no deliberate effort to build a passage between reality and fantasy. There is no marked entrance to her fantastical realm. Her characters do not require a planned process to freely roam between real and unreal scenes. She provides no explanation, no justification – these transitions simply come naturally in her captivating plays.

In *Night Picture of Rain Sound,* the main character, a library custodian named Adam Cloud, reads Shakespeare's *Romeo and Juliet*. Suddenly, he finds himself in the pages of the book itself, talking to Juliet in person, debating issues of his reality. Later, as Adam finishes another novel, the heroine knocks on the door of his studio, and he finds himself meddling in the very real affairs of these fictional characters.

Just as Adam questions: "Where is the line? Was there ever a line? Between time? Between space? Between circumstance?" This dreamlike theme reverberates throughout Joo's work.

Clone 1001 takes place in a vividly painted Dystopian world that does not, but could very well in the future, exist. *Zero*'s stage is set in an imaginary prison. *Vagabonds: Death to Anti-Romance* leaps between time periods without hesitation. Joo masterfully arranges elements of time and space in a unique fashion, seamlessly creating a link to reality.

Within her lawlessly free dramatic form, Joo gently poses the question of how we, the reader or audience, should define reality. Is our reality limited to what we can see and feel? She takes the philosophical challenge and yanks the door wide open for debate.

Accordingly, the audience is challenged to view and examine the world from a different perspective in the fluidity of Joo's reality. We are led to admit that the world is indeed not a straightforward or simple place. A single reality is deeply interwoven with a vast number of elements, and rests not on a single layer, but upon infinite layers of overlapping worlds.

At the same time, Joo's plays deliver hope, often hinting at the rekindling of a new life that could have been extinguished. *Clone 1001* and *Night Picture of Rain Sound* both end by suggesting an imminent new kind of human and a transformation into a new life.

Zero implies an esoteric world where transcendent freedom may be attained. Even in *Vagabonds: Death to Anti-Romance* set in a barren wasteland where books no longer exist, a new cycle for human life to survive and thrive emerges.

One may suggest that Joo finds salvation in humanistic values - literature, art, and perhaps even love. Yet, despite her choice of profound themes, she carries her work forward with a bright and cheerful touch. They are neither gloomy nor grim, capable of relating and resonating with multiple generations of different age groups. She crafts scenes with a quirky, fresh impact resembling short-form media in a delectably imaginative world. This, indeed, is what attracts the audience to the theatrical world of Sue Ja Joo, the driving force and foundation of her artistic universe.

PREFACE

To me, a play is like a dream that is dreamed in broad daylight. The outside world darkens, but the neurons in my brain lighten, and I always fall into a strange state. When the play is over, I often feel the outside reality must be the false one, and what I experience in my mind is real. It may sound like social escapism, but I am convinced that the reality we live in is just one out of many realities.

This kind of perspective is reflected in all of my plays: *Night Picture of Rain Sound* is about the boundary between the experience of reading and actual reality. At the core is the idea that reading a book is like entering a dream-like painting. A book is, in essence, a person in a different form. So I think the boundary between our imagination and real actions is ambiguous.

Clone 1001 explores the age-old struggle between science and religion. In order to reconcile these two forces, the main character clone is named 'Art'. The play *Zero* echoes Hamlet's saying, "O God, I could be bounded in a nutshell and count myself a King of infinite space".

Vagabonds: Death to Anti-Romance is a Korean musical that deals with the everlasting theme of Utopia. In this play, I boldly insist that there exists no age, nor time; the only thing left in this world is nothing but the word 'zero'. To that, I want to add the word 'love'.

The audience is the ultimate one who holds God's eye, and I bow to exit. I leave the interpretation of my plays to them.

I would like to express my boundless gratitude to Bruce Blanshard, who created the one and only marvellous book cover, and poet Susan Blanshard, who has offered me such immeasurable help.

—Sue Ja Joo

O God, I could be bounded in a nutshell
and count myself a King of infinite space...

—***William Shakespeare***

ZERO

THE PLAYERS

LIFER
Frail old man, Inmate number 9000

GUARD
Large man with a lame leg

BILLY
Young man in his twenties, Inmate number 1234

WALLY
Man in his thirties, Inmate number 317

HOLLINGSWORTH
Man in his forties, Inmate number 666

SCENE 1

(Center of the stage lights up, showing a prison cell with LIFER sitting by himself. He seems like a ghost – expressionless and still. From stage right, in the darkness, the chattering and whooping of a monkeys are heard, along with the sound of banging against metal prison bars. From stage left, in the darkness, a wolf howls and chains rattle)

(Footsteps are heard, uneven sounds of a limp coming from the gait of the GUARD, who enters, dragging his leg, swinging his baton. He is followed by BILLY, who is in handcuffs, head hanging low. As they enter the cell, BILLY lifts his head to look around. He notices the dark figure, LIFER, and reels back in surprise)

BILLY

What the hell!

(LIFER sits in silence)

BILLY

(steps backwards, raises his arms to shield himself, his eyes dart around the room)

What the hell? Man, beast?
Whatever you are, answer me!

GUARD

What's gotten your knickers in a twist?

(looks around and sees LIFER)

Oh him…? Yeah… that old man has been here…

(adjusts the brim of his hat)

well, forever.

BILLY

And I thought I was seeing ghosts.

LIFER

I… am a person.

BILLY

Might as well be a ghost.

LIFER

I… am a living, breathing person.

BILLY

(smirks in a hostile manner, pins LIFER against the wall then sneers in his face)

What did you say, old man?

(GUARD frees BILLY from handcuffs without interfering in the altercation, then turns around tucking the handcuffs in his belt. He casually walks out of the prison cell and locks the door behind him)

GUARD

Well, you two boys be good now! Don't make me come down here, you hear?

(Animal noises echo through the prison. BILLY paces back and forth)

LIFER

So, tell me. What lands a young man like yourself in a place like this?

BILLY

Oh, you know, nothing much. Larceny, extortion, fraud, assault, rape, murder, escape from custody… just to name a few.

LIFER

The whole package! Well, one way or another, we're all guilty.

BILLY

What brings you here, ghost man?

LIFER

Oh, I don't even remember. It's been a long time.

BILLY

Too long, by the looks of it.

LIFER

Perhaps. Have you looked in the mirror recently though?

BILLY

(turns and launches at LIFER again)

The hell you say, ghost man?

(LIFER slowly sits down in his spot, without a word. BILLY resumes his nervous pacing)

LIFER

Have you got a name?

BILLY

(lays on the ground, arms behind his head)

You're chatty for a ghost man, you know? Even if I had a name, it would be none of your business.

LIFER

That's a relief. We're a number in this place. One name or the other, we all go by the name of 'sinner'.

BILLY
(groaning)

This crap is getting real old, real fast!

LIFER

Here's my number. You can see it, right? Right on my chest.

BILLY
(looks down at LIFER's chest)

What, zero… zero… zero?

LIFER

Look again, it's nine, zero, zero, zero.

BILLY

What made-up inmate number is that? You're kidding, right?

LIFER

I kid you not!

(pounds on his chest)

Look, this void right here—zero, nil, zilch!

I've still got my work cut out for me, which is why I still have the nine, but one day, I'll get there, to a true zero, zero, zero, zero!

BILLY

(turns his back, shaking his head)

Like I care... zero, schmero.

LIFER

(walks around to face BILLY, and looks down at his chest)

Hmm, let's take a look, shall we... I see you are number one, two, three, four. Good, in fact, great! What an excellent choice.

BILLY

What are you talking about? I had no say in this.

LIFER

Nonsense, you always have a say, always!

BILLY

I had nothing to do with it.

LIFER

Really? Take a good look at yourself.

BILLY

I just wore whatever that guard told me to wear…

(looks down at his chest, sheepishly)

I mean, what is this bullshit number 1234 anyway?

LIFER

Now look inmate number 1234! There's no point blaming destiny.

BILLY

What'd you say? Destiny?

LIFER

That's right. Destiny.

BILLY

I'm getting real tired of your bullshit. Who cares about...

(points at his inmate number)

A NUMBER?
Just shut up and leave me alone old man, will you?

(BILLY's shouting seems to rile up the animals in the neighboring cells. The howling and screeching noises get louder and louder)

BILLY

(abruptly sits up)

What was that noise?

LIFER

What?

(pointing to the right side, sounding like a monkey)

That eek-eek-EEK!

(pointing to the left side, howling like a wolf)

Or that woo-oo?

BILLY

(nods, slowly)

I mean… what the…?

LIFER

Doesn't sound like beasts to me… 1234, I'll go take a look.

(LIFER walks towards the front of the cell and looks left, then right, pauses before speaking)

Yup, only humans in here.

BILLY

You're kidding me.

LIFER

I kid you not. You just haven't been listening. Perhaps you need to see for yourself.

BILLY

You sure we're in prison?

LIFER

I'm sure this is a prison.

BILLY

Sounds like a zoo, smells like a zoo!

LIFER

What matters is this cell we are in right now. No need to tune in to what's out there.

BILLY

What the hell? It's grimy out there in the world but in here? Ha! We get to be chained up with animals!

LIFER

I don't see it that way.

(BILLY walks up to the front of the cell, pressing his face as far as he can against the metal bars, looking left and right. With each turn, the lights go out, one by one)

BILLY

Damn it, I can't see anything. I can hear it, though!

LIFER

Definitely?

BILLY

The sounds. The smells. On the right, it must be a monkey. And I'm pretty sure the left is... a wolf.

LIFER

There are men out there that sound and smell like that.

BILLY

Bullshit! I know one when I see one. There lies a clear line between man and beast.

LIFER

Can you be so sure?

BILLY

For sure, for sure.

LIFER

So, you believe what you see? Do you listen to what you hear?

(BILLY, still confused, looks left and right. Another light goes out, and everything goes silent. In the dark, he returns to where he was laying before and lays down. The animal noises start again)

BILLY

(jumping back up)

Who's playing with me, who is it? I don't see anything, but I hear it, I definitely hear it!

LIFER

Look, 1234. That's just how it is. There are things you can see that don't exist. Things you can hear but cannot find. It's just...how... it is.

BILLY

You may say you're a zero, but you're full of crap.

LIFER

Come closer.

(BILLY approaches)

That's right, over here. I'll tell you the truth... those things you hear and smell. They're not beasts, nor human. They're simply... illusions.

BILLY
(skeptically)

Illusions?

LIFER
(with certainty)

Illusions.

BILLY

Should've known a ghost man would say nothing but hot air. Must be nice and full, with all that bullshit you're feeding yourself, ghost man. I, on the other hand, am starving!

LIFER

Well, those beasts you speak of are not those to hunt for food. In a way, they are our friends.

BILLY

Oh, just shut up already! When is that food cart coming?

LIFER

Soon enough, it'll be here. You're simply too hungry to recognize what is before you.

(The sound of a food cart, wheels rolling, can be heard off stage. GUARD's voice booms)

GUARD
(voice only)

Hey! Have we all been good little boys? Here, here my little piggies, it's food time!

LIFER

You see, 1234! I told you the food was on its way.

BILLY
(scoffs)

Congratulations, you can tell the future.

(Loud animal noises from neighboring cells. BILLY flinches)

LIFER
(notices BILLY flinching)

Not to worry, 1234. Nothing to fear. We're all family in here.

GUARD
(voice only)

Here, here! Get those paws on this grub while it's hot!

BILLY

I guess the animals get something to eat as well? Well, that's a surprise.

LIFER

We'll get ours when the time is right.

(GUARD enters, pushing a cart full of food. He throws a chunk of meat towards the wolf's cell. He throws a banana towards the monkey's cell. He throws a thin slice of toast each at LIFER and BILLY. He then exits whistling a tune)

BILLY

What's all this? Might as well be a piece of paper, this thin, stale, piece of toast! The beasts get steak and fruit, and what do we humans get? This is discrimination!

LIFER

Man shall not live by bread alone.

BILLY

Why, he sure shall! Man needs bread to live, one crumb after the other! This...

(holds up his slice of toast)

starts wars—it can bring a man to his knees, and make a man become his worst possible self! All for some stale bread!

LIFER

Could be right. Most likely wrong. One way or another, we're all wrong.

BILLY
(groans loudly)

I was sick and tired of it all out there! Now I get to do the same in here!

LIFER

Ah, forgive me, 1234! Whether it's the bread we eat or the words we say, we need to give ourselves something to go on… one way or another.

(They sit in silence, chewing on their slices of toast. The animal noises grow, then fade out. GUARD enters, whistling again, followed by WALLY and HOLLINGSWORTH)

LIFER
(speaks in a cheerful tone)

Welcome everyone! Make yourselves at home!

GUARD

Well, well, well. We haven't had a full house in a while!

LIFER

It must be getting bad out there, seeing so many of us in here!

GUARD
(mumbles)

Pointing fingers at the world now, are we?

LIFER

Well, we all need somebody to blame.

GUARD

It's a nasty habit, I say.

LIFER

Yessir!

GUARD
(starts to walk out, pauses, looks back at the new group and shouts)

Now you behave yourselves, you hear? If I hear a squeak from you guys? Believe me when I say, I'll make damn sure you won't be squeaking anymore!

ALL FOUR PRISONERS
(in unison)

Yessir!

(GUARD exits. WALLY walks forward, exploring his new cell, swinging from corner to corner in a monkey-like fashion)

BILLY

Will you look at that? This fool looks like a monkey!

WALLY

A monkey? Why do I take offense to that? I'm only here with you scumbags thanks to a glitch in the system, but compared to you lot? I'm a damn prince! So, bow down to Wally, the prince of Wall Street!

BILLY

Looks like a monkey, sounds like a monkey.

WALLY

(looks BILLY up and down and scoffs)

Looks like a loser, sounds like a loser. You most definitely don't come from money, honey, seeing that you've never heard of the great Wally of Wall Street. If you've ever set foot in the financial district, you would've heard of me.

(BILLY has already lost interest in WALLY, and walks over to HOLLINGSWORTH, while he still takes bites out of his slice of toast. HOLLINGSWORTH simply stares up at the ceiling, with an arrogant smirk on his face)

BILLY

Where have I seen this idiot before?

HOLLINGSWORTH

(smugly)

I'm sure you have somewhere. I'm quite famous.

BILLY

With that face? Let me guess...

(sings in HOLLINGSWORTH's face)

Who's afraid of the big bad wolf? The big bad wolf? The big bad wolf?

LIFER

As I said, 1234, it's hard to tell the man from the beast!

BILLY

(still keeping his eyes on HOLLINGSWORTH, he nods)

That you were right, old man!

LIFER

Hey, 1234! With your young, bright eyes, pray do tell, what are the numbers written across the chests of our new friends?

BILLY

(walks back to WALLY and scans his chest)

Hm. This one has an odd one. What is this… L… I… E… LIE? Is this some joke? Oh wait, my bad, it's upside down, it's 317.

LIFER

Upside down, you say? Why, what a silly-willy-Wally you must be. What about the big man?

BILLY

(walks towards HOLLINGSWORTH, looks at inmate's number)

Speak of the devil! This one is number 666!

LIFER

Astonishing… six, six, six, you say?
You must have quite the rap sheet, my dear scoundrel! Hopefully, the day will come when those sixes turn into zeros. Might be the day the world comes to an end, but it'll come eventually!

The world is full of us scoundrels. Living in both the black and white. Some are known as heroes, and some are known as gentlemen. Some are fathers, some are mothers. Perhaps

even children, if they act childish.
You don't need to go to court to be a criminal.

HOLLINGSWORTH

Shut that filthy mouth of yours! Who do you think you are, calling me a scoundrel?

LIFER

Are you not?

HOLLINGSWORTH

Damn well not!

BILLY

If you're not, why are you here?

HOLLINGSWORTH

I may have been accused of embezzlement, but I am no scoundrel. Never have been!

BILLY

Never say never. And never trust a man who says never. Moving on.

(turns towards WALLY)

Oh, monkey Wally, you! To what do we owe the pleasure?

WALLY

Well—I'm no scoundrel either!

BILLY

(speaks sarcastically to LIFER)

Sounds like we don't have any scoundrels in here! What a great place to be, chock-full of innocence!

(mumbles to himself)

A chock-full of excuses, I say.

LIFER

Now, now, 1234. It's not all black and white. For as long as I've lived, I have yet to see a villain who called himself one. Not out there, not in here. In fact, when I do meet one, I'll gladly bow down to that man and kiss his vile feet!

HOLLINGSWORTH

(scoffs)

Seems like a scoundrel can only see scoundrels.

LIFER

Good point. Whether that point is for you, or against you, now that's a good question.

HOLLINGSWORTH

I only make good points, great points.
Perhaps you've seen me on TV before.
They call me the prophet of our generation!

BILLY

Oh, shut up, you crook!

LIFER

A delusional one, this one.

BILLY

Nobody is getting swindled here!

HOLLINGSWORTH

How dare you speak to me like that?
You son of a...

BILLY

(with an intimidating snarl)

What?

(gets in HOLLINGSWORTH's face, staring him down)

LIFER

Now, this is a place where we are free of age, of status. There is no point in creating a hierarchy here.

BILLY

(without breaking eye contact with HOLLINGSWORTH)

Age is just a number, dwag.

WALLY

(in a high-pitched voice)

There, there, there lovers, this is just sad to watch. Age might be a number, but time? Time is gold! Gold, platinum, diamonds!

(stroking his neck and arm as if stroking imaginary jewelry)

And diamonds are Wally's very... best... FRIEND!

BILLY

The monkey goes for the money!

HOLLINGSWORTH

In the name of God! Who do you think you are?

(WALLY and HOLLINGSWORTH shove BILLY forcefully. The three prisoners start shoving each other back and forth. GUARD enters, swinging his baton in the air)

GUARD

Is that a squeak I hear?
Did I not warn you!

(The four prisoners scramble into line and stand up straight. GUARD walks up and down the line, twirling the baton)

GUARD

Can you see, with those beady dimwit eyes of yours, what is in my hands?

ALL FOUR PRISONERS

(in unison)

Yessir!

GUARD

I'm sure you remember, with your wretched bodies, what it feels like to be beaten to the bone with this bad boy, am I right?

ALL FOUR PRISONERS

(in unison)

Yessir!

GUARD

Attention!

ALL FOUR PRISONERS

(standing up straight, in unison)

Yessir!

GUARD

Down!

ALL FOUR PRISONERS
(getting into plank position, in unison)

Yessir!

GUARD

If I see a flinch, the tiniest movement, all of you will get to remember what this baton tastes like, you hear?

ALL FOUR PRISONERS
(maintaining their positions)

Yessir!

GUARD

Now you are going to stay here, and keep your beady dimwit eyes shut till the sun rises tomorrow, you hear?

ALL FOUR PRISONERS
(in unison)

Yessir!

GUARD

Now lie down, right where you are, and go to sleep. I don't want to see that you've moved an inch further than the width of the coffin we'll bury you in. You hear?

ALL FOUR PRISONERS

Yessir, thank you, sir!

(One by one, the prisoners flip over and lay in line, packed like sardines. Lights fade out)

(Soon after, only the faint sound of snoring is heard in the darkness. A soft snoring from BILLY, a quiet wolf-like growl from HOLLINGSWORTH, and occasional sleep talk, like monkey chatter, from WALLY)

LIGHTS OUT

SCENE 2

(A crescent moon between metal bars lights up the prison walls, suggesting that it's the middle of the night. The cell is eerily quiet, most of its inmates are fast asleep, laying single file, except for LIFER. LIFER sits cross-legged and motionless, with the moonlight shining against the back of his head. The faint sound of a woman's singing is heard. Her voice comes and goes like the wind)

LIFER
(softly)

Is it… is it you?

(A woman appears at the back of the stage, adorned with bird feathers. Singing a repetitive, haunting yet beautiful tune, she appears and disappears from the stage, as if she is a fragment of a distant memory, hidden in the deep forest of one's unconsciousness)

(The image of a young man appears in another corner, at the back of the stage. The young man is wearing a mask and is dressed in

an evening suit, yet his frail frame reminds one of a young LIFER. He leans against a lifeless tree, looking as if he is in pain)

LIFER

How long will you do this to me? Till the day they burn my flesh and bury my bones?

(lets out a sad moan that turns into sobs, as the woman's singing amplifies)

After all this time... you refuse to let go, or loosen your fingers from around my neck.

(As the sound of singing fades out, indiscernible shadows fly past behind LIFER's back. Like birds! Like ghosts!)

LIFER

Oh, what now? Oh, not you lot!

(Shadows rise and fly up above the stage, swarming above LIFER in a frenzied circle. No longer is beautiful singing to be heard, just shrieks and squawks of terror)

LIFER

Speak to me! What do you ask of me? Why, may I ask, why do you haunt me so?

(Shadows jeer and sneer, ferociously)

LIFER

I refuse to let you in, I refuse to kneel! End
this endless tormenting and leave me alone,
let me be!

(cries out and shakes his head)

What have I done to earn such anguish?
Why am I the one to blame, the bad guy,
the one that deserves to burn in this hell?
In this hell of a world, why was I singled out?

(Shadows shriek and scream viciously, as they loom larger. One streaks past LIFER, scratching his face, leaving blood trickling down his cheek)

LIFER

(brushes the blood off his cheek and laughs in disbelief)

Ha... haha... even you up there?
Who are you to call me such nasty, vile
names? Who are you to loathe me, to curse
me with venomous hatred? Just finish me
now, this minute, free me of these shackles!

(Shadows swarm and surround LIFER, attacking him as if bees stinging, birds pecking, beasts tearing away his flesh. The more he screams in pain, the louder the shadows shriek)

LIFER

(crying out loud)

Have it your way! Claw at my skin, feast on my flesh! Do as you please! I surrender, I kneel at your feet. I am unworthy of living, of dying, of anything! I am the bad guy, the one that should've died! I know nothing but myself, I know nothing but evil, I know… I know nothing!

(The woman reappears from backstage, as the shadows fade away. The shrieks fade out and the woman's eerie, yet serene, singing is heard again)

LIFER

Has it been forty years now? Forty miserable years. Death, the easy way out, the only way out. The only way of redemption. With every smash of my head against the wall. With every noose around my neck. I thought death would cleanse me… but alas, even death, the only choice I thought I had, was not mine to make. I had mistakenly believed everything was taken from me, yet I could rid myself of nothing. Not my past, my guilt,
my sins… not even my body, this piece of flesh. How could I wash away who I was, when I couldn't see a way to make amends or a way to be forgiven?

(The woman folds her arms like a bird folds its wings. The shadow of the young man reappears, leaning against the shadow of a barren tree)

LIFER

Time passed, no, flowed like the river.

(looks down at his fists)

These fists haven't punched another man since.

(opens his fists and stares at his palms)

These hands haven't held a knife since.

(puts his palms together in prayer)

Now, they pray. Pray for this world. While my body is older than the one you used to know, it belongs to you completely.

(kneels)

Yours to bite into. Yours to tear apart. Yours to shred into pieces. Utterly, unconditionally… yours.

(LIFER bows in surrender as everything else fades away, till only the faint lullaby-like singing of the woman is heard from far away)

(The rest of the prisoners snore, softly. LIFER is back at the end of the line, sitting cross-legged. Moonlight shines on the back of his head. Slowly, the light fades out, till only a crescent moon behind bars on the prison wall is seen. Then the shadow of the bars fades out slowly, till all that is seen is the crescent moon)

LIGHTS OUT

SCENE 3

(Early dawn)

(Everybody else is still asleep. LIFER stands up from his seat, walks towards the center of the room, turns to, face the east)

(On the right side of the prison cell a video montage is projected against the wall. The video is of climate change: natural disasters, destruction of rainforests, animals becoming extinct, melting polar caps etc)

LIFER

Gods of the East, who rise with the sun
and hold the power of light. Please guide us,
the arrogant humans, away from the path
of sinfulness and greed. Away from the path
of destroying our forests, our fields, our
livelihood. Away from the path of gluttonous

waste that fills our oceans, our lands, and our future. Guide us away from the path of annihilation. Enlighten us towards our salvation.

(Thunder claps loudly as if it approves of such prayers)

(LIFER turns facing the west. A new video montage is projected against the west wall of the prison cell, showing scenes of war and violence)

LIFER

Gods of the West, where the Goddess of Peace lays to rest. Forgive us for building a world of hatred and war. For choosing to act with violence, over using words of kindness. For wiping out our pasts with malice and filling our futures with pain.

Help us control this animosity, and bring peace to us reprehensible humans.

(Heavy rain falls as if the skies weep for such prayers)

(LIFER turns and faces the north, no video on the wall, just darkness)

LIFER

Gods of the North, those who watch over us in the darkness. Free us from the avarice that obscures our hearts, and the ignorance that cloaks our eyes. Free us from the prisons we shackle ourselves in.

(The earth shakes in unison as if it agrees. The prison cell walls move and shake with the earthquake)

LIFER
(turns to face the audience)

Gods of the South, the audience of our daily lives, who watch over us with such grace.

(GUARD appears amongst the audience. Walks down the aisle, towards the stage)

GUARD
(sings in a quiet sing-song voice)

Oh. Good morning to you, Inmate nine-oh-oh-oh.

LIFER
(falls back, surprised)

Goodness me! Who… who's there?

GUARD
(chuckles)

Relax, it's just me! Did you get some sleep?

LIFER

You almost put me to sleep for good! I didn't see you there!

GUARD

Well, I apologize for not being one of the gods you've been waiting for.

LIFER

(clears his throat)

Why are you here so early anyway? Do you need something from me? Did the wifey kick you out again?

GUARD

(sheepishly)

I mean… not really… no…

LIFER

What, have you come to play cards again? At this hour?

GUARD

(indicates dismissively)

Never mind! Just never mind me!

LIFER

(checks on sleeping cellmates)

Shut up before you wake somebody up.

GUARD

Oh, you don't have to worry about that. I seasoned their dinner with an extra something… a little something to help them sleep.

(pauses to listen to animals snoring)

Okay yeah, we're good. So anyway, old man, listen up. I thought you might appreciate a heads-up.

LIFER

(leans in)

Well, enough with the heads-up, get to the point!

GUARD

You might want to keep an eye on your new… roommate.

LIFER

Which one? The monkey?

GUARD

(shaking his head)

No, not the ape.

LIFER

What then, the wolf?

GUARD

(shakes his head)

Nope, not the hound…

LIFER

Who, the kid?

(points at BILLY)

What about him?
Honestly, he pulls at the heartstrings a bit, you know what I mean?

GUARD

Oh, I do. Kid's got quite the story. Was in and out of the system since he was ten but finally got sentenced to life without parole. He may look like a poor kid, but he's got a short fuse on him, that one! I'd watch out if I were you. Now that he's a lifer, he may want to… end it… if you know what I mean.

LIFER

What is he in for anyway?

GUARD

I just told you, he's in for life, like you.

LIFER

For what?

GUARD

Arson.

LIFER

What'd he burn down to burn down his future?

GUARD

Wood.

LIFER

Everything is made of wood.

GUARD

Yup… even houses. Very… important houses.

LIFER

(realizes what happened)

Oh… that house.

GUARD

The kid didn't stop there either. He could've laid low and gone into hiding, but he had to come back and set fire to all the top media networks. They caught him raving about how he had to burn the source of it all, how he had to cut out the core of the rotten intel going out into the world. Quite the revolutionist we got here.

LIFER

So much hate. So little hope.

GUARD

So little wisdom. Little to no hope. Perhaps he'll have a chance if you show him the ropes.

(The two stop talking for a second and walk over to look down at BILLY's sleeping face. Then they look up and face each other)

LIFER

(in an upbeat tone)

Anyhow. Hey, next time we play cards, no more cheating, you hear?

GUARD

(jokingly makes out he's offended)

How dare you, I play fair and square!

LIFER

Fair and square, my ass.

GUARD

Hey, hey, Inmate nine-oh-oh-oh. You better watch yourself! Remember who you're talking to!

LIFER

Oh, now you pull rank?
This is why the system will never improve. Fine, suit yourself. I don't have to play cards with you. I have better things to do with my time!

GUARD
(scoffs)

And what are you going to do with all that precious time, you got places to go?

LIFER

You'd think you were born yesterday!
Need I spell it out for you? I may not own much, but I still am the owner of my own time! I have no future to hope for, hence nothing to fear—I truly am a free man! My only concern is for the health and well-being of the earth we stand on.

GUARD
(rolling his eyes)

Uh-huh, uh-huh, whatever.
Look, I don't have the time to listen to one of your rants again. I'm taking my free ass out of here. I'll see you later when the sun comes up!

LIFER

(waves GUARD away)

Fine, fine, farewell!

GUARD

(starts to walk away, but stops at the door and looks back)

By the way… be careful what you pray for, yeah? Somebody up there might be… listening.

LIFER

Well, that's just terrifying now, isn't it?

LIGHTS OUT

SCENE 4

(Daylight breaks)

(A loud alarm sounds throughout the prison cell, time for the prisoners to wake up. Lights come up. The four prisoners stand in line, blankly staring at the audience)

(Rhythmical music plays as the prisoners get ready for the morning, miming in beat with the music. LIFER mimes brushing his teeth, passes the toothbrush to HOLLINGSWORTH, who brushes his teeth and passes the same toothbrush to WALLY. WALLY repeats the same and passes the toothbrush on to BILLY. BILLY scowls and throws the toothbrush into the corner, in disgust)

(LIFER mimes washing his face in a small plastic wash basin. He passes the basin to HOLLINGSWORTH, who washes his face and passes the basin onto WALLY. WALLY washes his face and passes the basin to BILLY. BILLY pours the water over his head, shaking it off like a dog, and throws the basin on the floor)

(LIFER mimes taking a comb, neatly combs his hair to the side and passes the comb to HOLLINGSWORTH. HOLLINGSWORTH does the same and passes the comb to WALLY, who repeats the same actions and passes the comb to BILLY. BILLY throws the comb without using it, then ruffles his hair vigorously)

(LIFER neatly buttons up his inmate uniform and brushes his inmate number. HOLLINGSWORTH and WALLY do the same in turn. BILLY looks down, shrugs, and does nothing)

(GUARD appears, pushing the food cart in for breakfast. He places a single breakfast tray in front of LIFER and retreats to the corner by the prison cell entrance. He stands back to observe)

(LIFER takes a couple of bites from the tray and passes it down to HOLLINGSWORTH. HOLLINGSWORTH does the same, passing the tray to WALLY, who repeats and passes the tray to BILLY. BILLY angrily flips the tray over onto the floor. The tray has already been emptied, so there is no food on the floor, just an empty tray and a plastic spoon. BILLY picks up the spoon and hides it in his pocket before anyone notices)

(As the morning routine ends, the music stops. All four prisoners stand like pillars, blankly staring into the distance. LIFER slowly sits down)

LIFER

Well, comrades. We've shared our names. Shared our daily bread. Shared a bed to sleep and wake next to one another. Now all that's left is to...

GUARD

(straightens his stance)

Share our secrets.

LIFER

You've come to the right place! Cell number 12 is a magical space, the place to take your 12-steps to rehabilitating your broken, crime-addicted soul. Only the worst of the worst land in this spot. It's been a while since this humble abode of ours has been so full of life—so full of sin.

Which one of you will be the first to open our little circle today by sharing the epic saga of your blood-tainted past?

GUARD

(laughing)

Oooh. I wanna hear, I wanna hear!

(The prisoners remain still, facing forward, expressionless, without uttering a word)

LIFER

(weaves between the other prisoners, looking them up and down)

Why the sudden loss of words?
Didn't quite picture you all as the quiet crowd. It's alright, this is a safe space. Be proud of who you are and come forward!
Come on, chin up, chest forward!
Be a man! Be the man!

GUARD

(playing along)

That's right, that's right! Be brave! Be honest! Be fun!

LIFER

They've taken everything from us, and I mean everything, but you know what they can't take? Our stories. Our legacy! So come forward, seize this opportunity to let it all out. While you're telling your stories, you may even surprise yourself, who knows?

(LIFER looks around, pausing for a second, waiting for volunteers)

Nobody? Alright, then random assignment it is. We'll start from... you!

(points at HOLLINGSWORTH)

Then go clockwise.

(The other prisoners do not respond, continuing to stare blankly)

LIFER

I'm waiting! Waiting to hear how you brought chaos to the world. Whose throat you had to slit. How many lies you had to tell? I'm waiting to hear all your secrets.

GUARD

Don't be afraid, nothing to fear! Again, this is a safe space. Confessionals aren't only in church! No man is perfect, it is our faults that make us stumble along the road. We're meant to screw up, over and over, till we reach the bottom of the fiery pit. It's all part of the journey!

So, step up! You're no longer in court, and not being judged!

BILLY
(abruptly steps forward)

You wanna hear what I've done? I'll tell you what I've...

LIFER
(cuts him off)

Whoa, whoa, whoa, there. There's an order to everything, even in this cramped prison cell, and it's not your turn yet.

(LIFER turns and points to HOLLINGSWORTH)

You! Cult leader! You're up first!

HOLLINGSWORTH

(trembles slightly)

God spoke through me.

GUARD

(interrupts the confession)

Whoa, whoa, whoa, there. I guess you're in here for lying because it seems like you just can't stop!

(HOLLINGSWORTH goes to WALLY, pulls him into the corner)

HOLLINGSWORTH

(whispers)

Why are we listening to the old man anyway?

WALLY

(whispers)

You know what, you're right! Who put him in charge?

(GUARD suspicious, swings his baton around, with a snarl)

GUARD

(without taking his eyes off the two)

Seems like some of us are going to need some inspiration.

LIFER

Seems like some of us have forgotten what freedom tastes like.

GUARD

(holds his baton up)

Now who's going to speak the truth before I beat it out of you bunch?

(HOLLINGSWORTH and WALLY stiffen for a second, then resume whispering in a conspiring manner. BILLY watches, and puts his hand in his pocket, reaching for the spoon he had smuggled)

WALLY

(whispers)

Something is up. The guard and the old man are teaming up.

HOLLINGSWORTH

(whispers)

It's not just me, right? Something seems off.

WALLY

(whispers)

Well, I'm gonna keep an eye on it.

HOLLINGSWORTH

Like how you're keeping an eye on my...

(looks around and whispers)

my stash?

WALLY

Shush!

(WALLY clears his throat, redirecting attention being paid to the two, steps forward reluctantly, to change the subject)

Fine, fine, I'll go first, we'll start small.
The world may point fingers at me, boo me,
and throw me in this hellhole but there was
a day when I was loved as much as a royal
prince! Look at me, such beauty and such
grace. I'm no thug or scumbag like the others.
I'm white-collar all the way.

HOLLINGSWORTH

As am I!

BILLY
(reacts angrily)

The hell I care if the collar around your neck is white or blue! Blue-blooded or not, when you slice that neck open, nothing but red will flow!

LIFER
(puts his hand up like a referee)

Inmate 1234, kid, that's another warning!
We've got rules in here, and in this safe space,
the number one rule is, we listen.

WALLY

(keeps nodding as if in agreement then speaks his duplicitous thoughts)

Yes, yes, yes. True words indeed! Even the filthiest of beasts have a pecking order, and disgusting cages like this have rules too. Rules are everywhere, even where I come from. The number one rule? Money is king. The rich only get richer, and anyone who says otherwise deserves to be dirt poor.

It's survival of the fittest, baby, and the fittest are the richest! Rich with money, yummy money, money, money. You know what else is money? Time. Time is glittering gold! And information! Information is the main currency.

Write this down honey, it's not like I'm going to be stuck in this hellhole for long anyway.

BILLY

Well, you deserve to be here. You're the reason why honest work gets you nowhere in life, why countless people are homeless, and why families are torn apart! Because of scumbags, or rather, monkeys like you who dance for the scumbags of the world!

WALLY

It's called capitalism, meathead, if you'd taken your head out of your ass long enough to put your head in a book. You'd know. It's the world we live in. Do you want me to spell it out for you? C-A-P-I-T...

BILLY

(launches at WALLY)

What did you just call me?

WALLY

(tauntingly)

I'm sorry, did I stutter, Meathead?

BILLY

(threatens WALLY's with his fist)

Let's see if you can say that again after I knock your teeth out!

HOLLINGSWORTH

(steps in)

Hey, no need for violence.

BILLY

Well you... you just shut your mouth! You are the real scumbag, the type of scumbag that this monkey dances for! Feeding off the rest of us!

HOLLINGSWORTH

I've done nothing of the sort.

WALLY

Me neither!

LIFER

Whoa, whoa, there 1234, hold on!
What is going on with you?
Why are you so angry?

(LIFER glances back at GUARD who had become bored, and dozed off, leaning on the cell bars)

BILLY

What makes me angry? Injustice, that's what pisses me off! Those scumbags who look down on us from their high perches, abusing us, and exploiting us, as if we're their slaves!

LIFER

The abuser and the abused?
The exploiter and the exploited?
Look here kid, it isn't black and white
anymore. Not in these times.

BILLY

Hate to break it to you, old man,
but you haven't been out there in a while,
and it's as black and white as night and day.

LIFER

The history of mankind may have been written simply for dramatic effect.

BILLY

I disagree. The written history of mankind is based on facts. On truth. The ugly truth.

LIFER

If you say so. What are you going to do about it?

BILLY

Oh, I'm going to do something about it! Can't just go slaving away to fill another man's pockets!

LIFER

But what else can you do? It's not that easy. The world won't fall into place like the numbers on your chest, Inmate 1234.

BILLY

Everything falls into place. Top before bottom, left before right and right before wrong!

LIFER

It's not that simple.

Think about it, 1234, look around. This place is crawling with people who tried to change the world. Who tried to turn injustice into justice and then disappeared into the shadows.

The history of mankind is based on facts, sure, but whose facts? Facts told by the abusers, the exploiters, the scumbags you speak of. Hitler wasn't the only bad guy. Alexander the Great, Napoleon the Genius, Genghis Khan the Legend?

All romantic words from history for scoundrels. Think about how many throats they had to slit; how many lies they had to tell! Do you think they cared about what was right or wrong?

BILLY

Yadda, yadda, yadda—quit yappin' your mouth off old man. Though it's the only thing that hasn't quit on you yet.

LIFER

Of course, you don't want to listen.
How could you listen to anyone when you're fixated on burning everything to the ground?
Does that change anything?
Hatred is a fool's game. All that burning rage will only drive you down further.

BILLY

Seems like you already know my story.
Fine, to hell with it. Burn it all to the ground!

LIFER

Burn what to the ground? Put your money where your mouth is, because from what I know, you didn't burn a damn thing.

(claps loudly)

Moving on!
Hollingsworth, you're up!

HOLLINGSWORTH
(steps forward)

Fine, to hell with it indeed, I will speak my truth! Let them cast the first stone at me. All I did was give the people what they wanted. It all came so easily. At first that is, the rest wasn't so easy. Why, you ask?

Everybody desperately wanted to believe in something. They wanted something solid, somebody real they could follow. They wanted to believe it was the real thing, and really, does such a thing exist?
They were all so tired of crippling fear and anxiety, and they needed somebody to step up for them. So, I did just that. I took their

heavy loads onto my shoulders and led them through the dark, I carried that cross! I earned my keep!

Don't you dare call it a cult, because from where I stand, my flock is my family.

WALLY

Hear, hear! We're all trying to help one another and live another day together!

(GUARD, who has been dozing off in the corner, stumbles and abruptly wakes himself up)

GUARD
(half-dazed)

And united we stand! No man can live alone. But of course… when it comes to taking blame… we can only point one finger at a time.

BILLY
(yelling, as in a protest)

Free the people. Bring down the man! We! Demand! Justice!

GUARD
(fully awake now)

Hold on Inmate 1234, when you take a pee, who can do it for you?

WALLY
(mockingly)

Ha, surely dick can do that job!

GUARD

First, you've got to know, is it your dick? Your manhood? Or is it just a dick amongst billions of other dicks in the world?

Now, I've got a matter of urgency... I've got to pee! See you later!

(GUARD waves dismissively, leaves the cell. HOLLINGSWORTH and WALLY return to the corner)

HOLLINGSWORTH
(whispers)

How did you get in here anyway?

WALLY
(whispers)

Oh, I have my ways.

HOLLINGSWORTH
(whispers)

Oh, you do you. As long as nobody catches on to my... investments.

WALLY

Oh, nobody is catching onto anything. Not out there, in here, or elsewhere. Unless you've told someone?

HOLLINGSWORTH

(pauses to think)

Hm. Nope, nobody that I can think of in my flock.

(BILLY keeps a keen eye on the whispering pair. Then he slowly walks over to them)

BILLY

Is there something going on here?
What's all this whispering about?
You two know each other?

WALLY

Accusations! I've never seen this man outside of these walls!

HOLLINGSWORTH

(crosses his arms in a giant X and shakes his head)

O-of course, w-what he said! We met in this very cell!

BILLY

(suspiciously)

Oh, something is most definitely going on here...

(BILLY walks up to them and sniffs around as if he's a police dog looking for clues. Billy sniffs WALLY a few times, breathes in deeply, then pauses)

Oh, oh, oh, this is good, I remember you, I know you!

WALLY

What the hell are you talking about... you hood rat?

BILLY

(laughing out loud)

Yes, yes, I remember the likes of you.

WALLY

And I detest the likes of you!

LIFER

Not to interrupt or anything, but what do you detest about him?

WALLY

Well... he stinks!

(pinching his nose)

Even his number stinks!

HOLLINGSWORTH

Agreed!

(pinching his nose in unison)

A foul order indeed!

LIFER

Must be the cages within these walls.

HOLLINGSWORTH

No, it's definitely the number 1234! The stench of poverty!

BILLY

Well, I can smell your bullshit from a mile away!

LIFER

Must be the animals within these walls.

BILLY

Don't you change the subject, I do know you and I do remember you! I'm sure you don't remember me; your kind never pays attention to our faces. But for us, the victims? We never forget the look of your guilt-ridden faces.

WALLY
(looks away)

I have no idea what you're talking about.

HOLLINGSWORTH
(turning in the same direction)

Same. No idea.

BILLY
(solemnly)

Codename Black Hornet. Over and out.

(WALLY and HOLLINGSWORTH freeze, stopping in their tracks as if they have seen a ghost)

BILLY

Now you know what I'm talking about.

(WALLY covers his eyes and starts shrieking like a monkey)

BILLY

What are the odds?

(WALLY continues to shriek like a monkey, jumping up and down slapping his face)

LIFER

What are the odds! We could do the math,

but I'll just jump ahead and say that nothing is impossible, and everything is possible. It's part of what makes life fun.

BILLY

Fun indeed. Such cruel fate, to meet me, of all people, in here, the direst of all places?

WALLY

You're the one! You're the reason why I'm here!

HOLLINGSWORTH
(speaks to WALLY)

He's the one? The one who took the weekly offering envelopes to the dumpster?

BILLY
(snarls at HOLLINGSWORTH)

Black Hornet in the flesh.

(WALLY covers his face with his hands and shrieks maniacally, like a crazed monkey)

HOLLINGSWORTH

What in god's name!

BILLY
(bangs on the cell bars shouting)

Guard! Where are you? Guard!

(WALLY and HOLLINGSWORTH rush over to silence BILLY. WALLY puts his hand over BILLY's mouth, and the three start to fight)

BILLY

Justice! I demand justice! Guard!

HOLLINGSWORTH

(between punches)

Haven't you heard what the Lord saith when it comes to snitches?

BILLY

(shouts out to the guard)

There's been a mistake! These two know each other! They're scheming together! I have proof! Solid proof!

WALLY

(holds the back of BILLY's neck, trying to keep him quiet, and whispers)

Look, it doesn't need to be like this, Hornet. C'mon. Tell us what you want.

BILLY

You know what I want?

(bangs on the metal bars loudly)

Justice!

LIFER

Hey, hey 1234, pull yourself together!
The law will take care of these two.

BILLY

What? Because the laws have taken care of everything so smoothly so far?

LIFER

Dura lex, sed lex... The law is harsh, but it's still the law.

BILLY

Shut the fuck up, old man.

(BILLY reveals the shank he carved out of the spoon and lunges towards WALLY and HOLLINGSWORTH. The three get re-entangled into a fight while lights flash)

(WALLY pries the shank out of BILLY's hands, and suddenly, everything moves in slow motion. As WALLY winds his arm back to drive the shank into BILLY, LIFER steps in between them. As the shank slices into LIFER's abdomen, time returns to normal... LIFER falls to the ground)

WALLY

(brushes the hair out of his eyes)

Is he dead?

HOLLINGSWORTH
(steps to WALLY's side)

I doubt it… Wait, is he?

BILLY
(calls through the cell bars for help)

Help! Guard! Anybody! Is anybody out there?

(BILLY kneels and holds LIFER's limp body, lets out a primal scream)

BILLY
(sobs)

Why would you do that old man, for what,
for a low life like me? A nobody?
Please tell me somebody is out there.
Up there... somewhere!
A man is dying in here... all for nothing!
Please help!

(BILLY's sobs, screams echo through the prison, sirens wail)

LIGHTS OUT

SCENE 5

(One week later)

(LIFER lays in the prison cell, recovering from his ordeal. BILLY sits next to him, watching with a worried look)

BILLY

You okay, old man?

(LIFER stays still, without a response)

BILLY

Say something, ghost man, will you?

LIFER
(eyes closed)

I'm not a ghost yet. A little peace would be nice, though.

BILLY

Sorry.

LIFER
(opens his eyes)

For what?

BILLY

Forgive me.

LIFER

For what? It's all water under the bridge. Speaking of… how long have I been out?

BILLY

A week or so.

LIFER

I mean, what time is it?

BILLY
(looks around, and shrugs)

Morning, I guess? It's not like they gave us a clock.

LIFER
(tries to sit up)

Another day that shall never return has

begun! Well, I've got things to do.

BILLY
(attempts to hold him down)

Nonsense, you need your rest.

LIFER

No, no, nonsense. I have an appointment to make.

BILLY
(looks around, and shrugs)

With whom? It's not like there's anyone else in here.

LIFER

Not an appointment with another human! Perhaps an appointment with myself! Perhaps an appointment with the wall!

BILLY
(gives a dubious look)

... you okay, old man? The wall?

LIFER

Not just the wall—these walls! North, East, South, West!

BILLY

You sure you're okay?

LIFER

My flesh may be in recovery, but my mind and soul are fully up and running!

(BILLY shakes his head and walks over to the cell wall. He runs his hand against the wall, feeling the texture)

BILLY

What's so special about these walls?
Do they talk to you or something?

LIFER

Not exactly in words. You see, when you pay your respects to these walls, they respect you back. As is the case with anything or anyone in life. You pay love back with love. Like a mirror. An echo.

BILLY

You sure you don't want to rest some more?

(shakes his head and looks back at the wall)

Yet… if what you're saying is true… shouldn't I be able to see it too?

LIFER

Do you ever listen? There's always more than what the eyes can see.

BILLY

Say what?

LIFER

Now lend me a hand, will you? I can't lie around here all day.

BILLY

If you say so.

(BILLY reaches out and LIFER grabs his hand. LIFER stands up with a groan. His ribcage is wrapped in bandages, with blood stains visible)

LIFER

What do you plan to do now?

BILLY

I want to follow you.

LIFER

Don't follow me!

BILLY

Why not?

LIFER

Be yourself. Do not be a follower. This world is full of predators. Never follow anyone.

BILLY

(looks around)

Again, it's just you and me in here, old man.

LIFER

Again, there's always more than the eyes can see! Maybe you should stop looking for what's out there and start looking at what's in...

(points at BILLY's chest)

there. Stop looking for somebody to follow and start following your gut. Alright, enough talk, I'm a busy man! I've got my routines to attend to, and walls to respect!

BILLY

So do I.

(LIFER and BILLY stand facing the audience)

(The same rhythmical music from the beginning of Act Four starts to play. LIFER and BILLY get ready for their morning, miming to the beat of the music)

(LIFER mimes brushing his teeth. He hands the toothbrush over to BILLY. BILLY brushes his teeth in the same manner, then tries to hand the toothbrush to the next person. When he realizes nobody is there, he puts the toothbrush in his jacket pocket)

(LIFER mimes washing his face in a small plastic wash basin. He passes the basin to BILLY, who washes his face in the same manner. He then holds the wash basin up and drinks the water, wiping his mouth as he sets the basin aside)

(LIFER takes a comb, neatly parts his hair to the side, and passes the comb to BILLY. BILLY neatly combs his hair to look exactly like LIFER's)

(LIFER neatly buttons up his inmate uniform and brushes off his inmate number. His inmate number has changed from '9000' to '0000'. Music pauses for a moment as the lights focus on the number. Music resumes when BILLY buttons up his inmate's uniform and pats the number on the inmate's chest. His number has gone from 1234 to 2468)

(Once their morning routine is over, the music ends, and the two men turn around to face the right side of the prison cell. As they kneel and pray, a video montage is projected against the wall. The video montage is of climate change: natural disasters, the destruction of the rainforest, animals becoming extinct, melting polar caps, and so on)

LIFER

Gods of the East, those who hold the suns
of all our tomorrows so tightly in your grasp.
Retrain those who would destroy our woods,
pollute our oceans, and slaughter our species
into extinction. Stop them from obliterating
our home, our earth, our sanctuary.

(Thunder claps loudly as if it approves of such prayers)

(LIFER and BILLY turn around towards the left side of the prison cell, facing the west. A new video montage is projected against the wall of the left side of the prison cell. The video montage shows scenes of war and violence)

LIFER

Gods of the West, those who light up the night skies with the moons of tomorrow. Show the light to those filled with darkness, those who speak through war crimes and respond with malice and violence. Those who are full of mistakes and misunderstandings. Light up their dark hearts. Blanket the world with the calm of night.

(Heavy rain falls as if the skies weep for such prayers)

(LIFER and BILLY turn towards the back, facing the north. There is no video montage, but unlike the darkness of before, stars shine in the night sky)

LIFER

Gods of the North, those who shine throughout the night sky. Outshine the avarice that obscures our hearts, the ignorance that cloaks our eyes. Shine throughout the prisons that we shackle ourselves to, and help us find our freedom.

(The earth shakes as if it agrees in unison. Bricks in the cell walls shift)

(LIFER and BILLY turn again, facing forward, towards the audience)

LIFER

Gods of the South, the audience of our daily lives, watch over us with your gracious eyes.

(From the South, where the audience sits, an earth-shaking sound slowly fades in. As the noise gets louder, the prison cell walls crack. The floor shakes, suddenly tilting to the side. The audience starts to participate, stamping their feet against the floor. As the stamping continues, the rumbling noise continues to ramp up, maximizing the earthquake effect on stage)

(LIFER and BILLY's jaws drop in awe, and the two turn to stare at each other)

BILLY

What on earth is happening?

LIFER

Life is happening, Inmate 1234, no 2468, oh whatever it is now! Life is giving you an answer, a chance to start over again!

BILLY
(eyes glisten with hope)

Come with me!

LIFER

Who, me?

BILLY

I don't see anyone else here!

LIFER
(shakes his head)

You go ahead now, get going! I'm fine here.

BILLY

Here? What on earth is left here for you?

LIFER

Committing a crime was enough punishment, there is no point in staying here, just waiting for a further sentence. Get going! Get moving!

BILLY

The same could be said for you as well. Come, join me!

LIFER

Go on without me. I may wish to be freed of

my flesh, but I do not ask to be freed of my shackles.

BILLY

Of course you do! Now, shut up old man, and get a move on!

LIFER

Freedom cannot be found for me out there anymore. I could be bound in a nutshell and count myself a king of infinite space!

BILLY

I will never understand what you talk about, old man.

LIFER

'Twas not I to speak such words, but Hamlet.

BILLY

Shamlet? Whoever said such a stupid saying!

LIFER

(laughs)

You'll learn one day! And to do so, you must leave right now! You are not running away; you are opening a new door.

BILLY
(fondly)

I will remember you.

LIFER

Then remember this: your only job now is to find happiness. Mark my words!

(BILLY walks towards LIFER to embrace him. LIFER pats BILLY's back with encouragement, and BILLY turns towards his freedom. LIFER waves him away)

LIFER

Get going!

BILLY

I will remember you forever!

(BILLY runs down to the audience and disappears amongst the crowd)

LIGHTS OUT

SCENE 6

(In the remains of the prison cell, shards of light shine through. What used to be greyscale and monotonous, now shines in a brilliance of triangle-shaped hues against the cracked prison walls)

(LIFER stands in the cell alone, staring blankly ahead. GUARD enters, carrying two chairs, a pack of playing cards tucked under his arm)

GUARD
(limps in)

Is the kid gone?

LIFER

Long gone.

GUARD

What'd I tell you? Be careful what you pray for. Am I right?

LIFER

(nods his head)

God may not be listening, but the walls did... after all.

GUARD

Should've gotten some sleep instead of wasting time praying.

LIFER

Must have been… meant to be.

GUARD

Must have been. Anyway. You've got a debt to settle, old man.

LIFER

If you say so.

(LIFER and GUARD sit on the chairs. They start to play cards)

GUARD

(deals the cards)

Alright, let's play. It's all we've got to look forward to.

LIFER

What, cards? Ha, maybe for you, but I've got more.

GUARD
(snorts)

As if! What more is there to life than these cards? This shuffled deck of unpredicted events? It's called gambling for a reason, nobody knows what's going to happen in life. Life is the ultimate gamble.

(flips over his cards one by one, revealing the numbers)
After number 1, do you always get number 2? Certainly not. One moment in life, you may be a ten, but the next moment you end up as a zero, zero, zero, zero... like yourself.
You may start with your ducks in a row, one, two, three, four... just to start over 2468 like the kid, you hear?

LIFER

I hear you.

GUARD

Damn right you do, I rule with an iron fist!

LIFER
(scoffs)

As if! Why don't you rule by example and play fair and square for once?

GUARD

Now, where's the fun in that?

LIFER

Perhaps you'll find some joy in an honest game.

GUARD

Speaking of honesty, why'd you let the kid go?

LIFER

It wasn't up to me.

GUARD

You sure about that?

LIFER

(exchanges a sneaky look with the audience)

It was out of my hands.

GUARD

Who's hiding the truth now?

LIFER

I hide nothing.

GUARD

I call your bluff! How could a few rumblings split open these walls?

LIFER

A butterfly could flap its wings and do a lot more.

GUARD

So, they say.

LIFER

Think about it. Who would be capable of opening a man-made door, locked by man himself? Who else would have the key, other than man? You? I wouldn't think so.

GUARD

Ooh, Uno!

(GUARD laughs as he tosses his last card on the table and gathers up the cards. In the distance, the animal sounds resume, with a monkey shrieking and a wolf howling)

LIFER

Wait! Why do I feel like I've been cheated again? You're one sneaky so-and-so!

GUARD

To be sneaky is a privilege, one that comes with power. Come to think of it, you've got one sneaky mouth on you, so maybe it's me who's being cheated!

(scoffs)

You're always the one talking about your infinite kingdom in this nutshell. Why did you tell the kid to make a run for it?

LIFER

I told him how my freedom couldn't be found out there, how I could count myself as a king of infinite space.

That is my truth. However, that doesn't mean it is his. He still has apologies to make out there, sins to atone for, and debts to settle.

GUARD

You'll pay the price within these walls! With this baton!

LIFER

He already paid the price when he committed the crime.

(GAURD and LIFER hold up their new set of cards, and glare at each other as if they are about to do battle)

GUARD

Settle down now, Inmate 9000… no, Inmate 0000. So, you think the kid will ever come back?

LIFER

Probably not. At least I hope not.

GUARD

Well, I on the other hand, certainly hope so! Once a crook, always a crook. He's going to come back! They always come back!

LIFER

(looking through his cards)

Once he tastes the sweet nectar of freedom, there's no turning back.

GUARD

Such a high and mighty believer. No wonder your ass is in this place. And the kid's ass will land right back in here someday, right back next to yours!

LIFER

We'll see about that.

GUARD

(slams his last card on the table)

Uno again!

(Animals cause a ruckus, in the background)

LIFER

Again? Can't be right.

GUARD

There is no right or wrong when you're playing games. Like you and your speeches - no rules, no order, no sense.

LIFER

You're the one making no sense.

GUARD

Why, it's not my job to make things easier for you! It makes sense if I say it does because I make the rules... and uno, again!

(A wolf howls in the distance. The lights dim slowly, as the sounds of wildlife get louder)

GUARD

There's only one thing all that noise could mean... sounds like you're getting company! Buckle up, old man, this group sounds wild!

LIFER

Me? Here? Why now?

GUARD

You're the one who stayed. Now it's time to take responsibility.

LIFER

Isn't it your responsibility to look after us?

GUARD

I may have the power. I may reap the benefits. This lord has no intentions of looking after you lot.

LIFER

Well, I applaud you for your courage to admit to your shortcomings. My lord! After all, you're trapped in here with us, all the same!

GUARD

And while we're all trapped in here, I'd keep an eye on those cards of yours.

LIFER
(looks down at his cards)

Oh yes, indeed, uno for me, finally!

GUARD

Ah, darn it, lost in the last round.

(The sound of wings flapping, echoes in the background)

GUARD

Well, it's not like you need the money anyway. So how about I make you a deal. What did that monkey-looking guy say, information is the main currency, am I right? Come closer, here's a little secret for you that money can't buy.

LIFER

I can hear you fine from here.

GUARD

As can the rest of the world! You want to hear the secret or not?

LIFER

Perhaps some secrets are better kept than shared.

GUARD

Oh, stop being so boring and come here.

(looks at the audience suspiciously)

Feels like we've got a lot of ears out there. Of course, we have no idea whether they're listening to—what they're hearing.

LIFER

Now, now guard. What's the point of ruling with an iron fist if you can't trust those under it?

GUARD

And what's the point of staying in here if you can't trust the iron hand that feeds you? Did those zeroes stand for nothing in the head? Or perhaps it stands for zilch in the heart?

LIFER

Head, heart, soul, flesh—think what you may. Now come clean and share this secret you speak of.

GUARD

Then come closer, and listen up. Your mind will be blown away by what I do know, and what I don't know. The truth of all truths is…

(whispers to LIFER, who shakes head in disbelief)

LIFER

You don't say.

GUARD

I do say. Have you gone deaf, old man? Come closer, Inmate 0000, lend me your ears.

(GUARD pulls LIFER closer and continues to whisper in his ear. LIFER's eyes widen, and his jaw drops)

GUARD
(steps back)

Isn't that the truth.

LIFER

Indeed.

GUARD

Now watch that rambling mouth of yours! This is a secret meant to be kept!

LIFER

You got it. My lips are sealed to the very end!

GUARD

Sealed or not, I'm going to keep an eye on you. You hear?

(GUARD exits into the background. LIFER steps forward, looking at the audience)

LIFER

If what I've heard is the truth… then… that's one unexpected truth indeed.

(LIFER looks up and points into the air, mouthing the word 'zero'. A dark spot appears around his finger, growing larger and larger, growing to cover the whole stage with darkness, till all fades to black)

LIGHTS OUT & CURTAIN

Everything you can imagine is real.

—***Pablo Picasso***

NIGHT PICTURE OF RAIN SOUND

THE PLAYERS

ADAM CLOUD
Young man who works as a library custodian

MOTHER
Adam's late mother

HEROINE
Woman in her early 30's

BOYFRIEND
Deadbeat musician

FETUS
Heroine's unborn child

JULIET
Character from William Shakespeare's Romeo and Juliet

THE SCENE

ACT I

Town Square in front of the City Library in the evening. It is raining, and the sound of falling rain is played throughout both acts. Props on the stage are disproportionally larger or smaller than life-size, creating a fantastical atmosphere. Amongst such props, on the left side of the stage, there is a giant closed book, the title Romeo and Juliet, written on its cover.

Upon entry, audience members are given a choice of 'trash' to take to the stage, such as food waste (stale bread, cold pizza slices), empty plastic bottles, crumpled newspapers, or torn books. Before sitting down, audience members are invited to walk up to the stage and litter it with their 'trash'.

ACT II

Adam Cloud's studio apartment, late at night. Dimly lit and ill-maintained. Books piled up from corner to corner, along with an old dirty futon in the middle of the room.

ACT I

SCENE 1

(A trash-ridden town square. ADAM CLOUD enters, wearing a utility jumpsuit and pulling a custodian's cart. He looks at the job ahead of him and sighs. He wedges the broomstick under his arm and fixes his hat, ready to work)

ADAM

Such waste.
Where does all this trash come from anyway?
Well, I guess I better get to work.

(starts sweeping trash into a pile)

Pray do tell your tales, trash of the streets…
what happened in this city today?

(ADAM sweeps busily. A small paperback falls from his chest pocket. He picks it up and brushes off the cover, examining the book as he puts his broom to the side)

ADAM

What a strange little thing, this tiny rectangle!
Just some paper and leather bound by staples
and glue. Yet, opening it unlocks a gateway to
an entire universe! And shutting it puts a nail
in the coffin.
How peculiar.

(flipping through the pages)

This little rectangle can both stop and speed
through time, amplify and silence emotions
and transport you to a different world.
How bewildering!

(ADAM walks across the stage reading the pages. As he reads, the giant book on the side of the stage opens, and the pages turn in sync with ADAM's reading. He pauses at a page and sits down on a bench. JULIET reads aloud)

JULIET

O Romeo, Romeo, wherefore art thou
Romeo?
Deny thy father and refuse thy name,
Or, if thou wilt not, be but sworn my love,
And I'll no longer be a Capulet
Tis but thy name that is my enemy.
Thou art thyself, though not a Montague.
What's Montague? It is nor hand, nor foot,
Nor arm, nor face. O, be some other name

Belonging to a man.
What's in a name? That which we call a rose
By any other word would smell as sweet.
So Romeo would, were he not Romeo called,
Retain that dear perfection which he owes
Without that title. Romeo, doff thy name,
And, for thy name, which is no part of thee,
Take all myself.

ADAM

How divine! How can one have such a precise grasp of human nature?
The Bard is my prophet, my priest, my king!

(turns another page in the book, and reads with a quizzical expression)

Did Romeo and Juliet truly love each other though? Enough to die for?
I mean, let's get real.
They barely knew each other.
My Bard might be a little off in his grasp of reality here.

JULIET

What's here?
A cup closed in my true love's hand?
Poison, I see, hath been his timeless end.
O churl, drunk all, and left no friendly drop
To help me after! I will kiss thy lips.

Haply some poison yet doth hang on them,
To make me die with a restorative.

(ADAM reads, turning to the last page. Lights flash. JULIET and ROMEO are now seen, in front of the giant book. ADAM looks up and turns his head towards the pair. ROMEO lays dead on the floor, with his head in JULIET's lap. JULIET is holding a dagger to her chest)

ADAM

Whoa, whoa, whoa there, hold it! Stop, I beg of you!

(JULIET pauses in surprise and looks towards ADAM across the stage)

ADAM

Is this truly what you want to end your life for? This… puppy love? Is this all you are worth? It's just… too much! Too much pressure, for everyone!
You can't leave us with such… a burden!

JULIET
(offended)

A burden?

ADAM

Why… oh why, would you choose death over… this attraction, infatuation, or whatever you think is love? What does your death solve?

JULIET

Pardon?

ADAM
(clears hroat, rambles on the go)

I mean… what would happen to… our society? I mean, look at the numbers! Every year we trade in our lives for worthless reasons! Suicide is the latest epidemic. It's a disease we need to eradicate by stepping up and taking responsibility!

JULIET

I must stop you right there.
Contrary to what you may think,
I do not choose death merely for love.

ADAM
(taken aback)

You don't?

JULIET

Of course not! And excuse me, but who are you exactly?

ADAM

(stuttering)

I-I-I'm just… a nobody. The janitor. The custodian. The clean-up guy in this library. B-b-but… I'm also a reader. An avid reader of the Bard's work!

JULIET

(raising her brow)

A reader?

ADAM

Oh, I apologize if I've overstepped my bounds. Yet I couldn't simply watch you…

(looking down at his feet in embarrassment)

such a beautiful young woman in her prime… to end her life in such a way! I ask… why must the reader only be on the receiving end of the story? We're readers, not bystanders!

These tales, these words, have such influence over us. We should be able to use such power as well.

I'm not saying we should change the plots or characters, but how I interpret and accept such information should be up to me, and only me.

(JULIET has already lost interest and turned her back on him, stroking Romeo's cheek)

ADAM

Please! Do not choose death.

JULIET

To choose life is to choose agony.

ADAM

Don't do this!

JULIET
(kisses ROMEO's deathly lips)

Thy lips are warm!

(lifts the dagger back to her heart)

Yea, noise? Then I'll be brief.

ADAM
(struggling to stop her)

Please... please don't Juliet. I beg of you.

JULIET
(ignoring ADAM)

O, happy dagger!

ADAM

Listen! Please! All you need to do is be... patient. Time heals all! At least that's where I've been. Sure, it feels like the end of the world, but it gets better! This too shall pass! So please... wait, just a little. For you. For me!

JULIET

You speak of minor setbacks in life. The emotional equivalent of a scratched knee. Romeo and my story... our saga... it's different.

ADAM
(scoffs)

How so?

JULIET

Ours is not a simple ballad of heartbreak. My sweet Romeo and I are fated to remain a symbol—the sacrificed; a tale of the pure, innocent blood of two lambs. All to put an end to a febrile hatred between two households. Destiny cannot be thwarted, and you certainly shall not diminish our blighted tale to a simple love story. Our story has been distorted and misrepresented.
Thou shalt search further, and deeper for the symbols this world is made of.

ADAM

(looks blankly ahead, in a daze)

Symbols.

JULIET

(holds dagger to her heart)

This is thy sheath. There rust and let me die.

(JULIET stabs herself in the heart and collapses over ROMEO's body. As she dies, the giant book cover closes, and the lights turn off. Screaming pierces the city square. A loud siren wails as an ambulance passes by with red lights flashing. ADAM follows the ambulance, like a man in a trance)

ADAM

Life. Death.

(lengthy pause)

Love. These are all… symbols? You… are a symbol. I… am I a symbol? All of this… the world as we know it… is it all a symbol?

(ADAM steps back in a fluster and confusion, clutching the paperback, close to his chest)

LIGHTS OUT

SCENE 2

(ADAM busily sweeps trash in the town square. The giant book from the previous scene has disappeared. As ADAM continues to work, head down, a scrolling video of the cityscape at night plays in the background)

(MOTHER enters from the shadows. She walks to ADAM, expecting her son to notice her immediately, yet when he does not notice, looks annoyed and offended. She snaps her fingers in ADAM's face to get his attention)

MOTHER

Adam Cloud! You almost swept me up with the rest of the trash!

ADAM

(jumps back in surprise)

Mother? What are you doing here?

MOTHER

What, a mother can't come to see her son at work?

ADAM

Is there something urgent?

MOTHER

Listen Adam… sweetie. It's my heart… it's heavy these days.

ADAM

With the place you're at now?

MOTHER

I'm telling you.

ADAM

Mother, I've got work to do.

MOTHER

What, the trash is in a hurry to go
somewhere? Priorities, Adam Cloud.
It's not like it's your job anyway.
Are you not a library janitor?

ADAM

Technically, yes.

MOTHER

Then why are you exerting yourself so much? It's not your responsibility.

ADAM

This is my responsibility. My contribution to society.

MOTHER

Your contri-... what, to what?

ADAM

My contribution to society, my share to be done. Somebody needs to clean the streets, and somebody needs to maintain order and balance, to keep this city from collapsing.

MOTHER

Must you be like this?

ADAM

I'm just doing my share.

MOTHER

(scoffs)

That's the dumbest thing I've ever heard.

ADAM

My job is to clean up trash, in the light, and in the dark. Whether you see the trash or not.

MOTHER

Oh, you're sweeping invisible trash now?

ADAM

One must take responsibility for what one can see. Our eyes only show us what we are capable of handling. It is the world's way.

MOTHER

(rolling her eyes)

I don't see the point.

ADAM

Mother, I like this job. Every day, I get to restore order to the world. Besides, I have time to read.

MOTHER

All that reading for what? It certainly isn't putting food on the table!

ADAM

Man doesn't live by bread alone, Mother. You have your own life, I mean, your own realm, and I have my life, let's leave it at that.

MOTHER

Well, somebody needs to knock some sense into you, and what kind of mother would I be

if I didn't make sure of it?
You have a diploma. Not just any diploma, a fancy J.D. You could've been a lawyer!
A Supreme Court judge!

ADAM

I don't want to judge others for a living. That is not what I intend to do, ever.

MOTHER

You know what I went through to put you through school? The days I spent in the shivering cold on the floor of that market selling fruit, so you could afford your fancy tuition. You're breaking my heart, kid!

ADAM

My life's purpose is to be with books, Mother.

MOTHER

(kicking the trash in frustration)

Ugh, when will you grow up? What's so wrong with the normal path—making an earnest living for the best life possible? What's so wrong with getting a desk job, getting paid? Everybody else does it!

There are people out there who would give an arm and leg to have a chance at the opportunities you've kicked out to the curb. Who are you to say that it's not a life worth living?

ADAM

It's not for everyone, Mother. Certainly not for me.

MOTHER

Adam, sweetie, you are my life's crowning achievement, the highlight of my time on earth. You know that, right? You can do better, right?

ADAM

If that is true, it's not much to brag about. You can't put that on me, Mother. We are not placed on this earth for somebody else.

(Lightning strikes and thunder roars)

MOTHER

For heaven's sake, what is going on?

ADAM

Sounds like rain.

MOTHER

(covering her head)

Ugh, well that's bad news for my hair. Alright, sounds like my time is just about up. So, do your mother a solid, sweetie; can you move me from the temple or not?

ADAM

What's wrong with the temple? They're supposed to be the best with Buddhist funerals.

MOTHER

The temple is fine. Fun, even. I'm just not... comfortable there anymore. Not with that senseless hag next door! I'll tell you what kid, people? They don't change. Nothing changes people, not even death! You'd think death is the one 'life-changing' event, but nope, not a chance!

ADAM

(shaking his head)

Mother, really...

MOTHER

I'm telling you! The stupid old hag that moved in next door! The stubborn old cow seethes at the sight of me... she can't leave me alone!

ADAM

What'd you do now, Mother...

MOTHER

What'd I do? Adam Cloud, you watch your mouth. I did nothing, nothing! She doesn't have and shouldn't have an issue with anything I've done—I've been perfectly pleasant and cordial with her.

The old bat was a devout Buddhist her whole life but dropped dead one day with nobody to shed a tear for her. Sad, right? All I did was try to play nice and be empathetic about it, but UGH! The bitter cow just decided to find all the hate within her and redirect it to a new target... on my back!

Here I am, just trying to get along with everyone—then she just starts spouting her mouth off and berating me. How dare I rest there, taking up precious space on the altar, when I'm a Christian. Not every soul up there is exactly a monk, lady! But does she care? Nope!

The new bitch on the block just had to assert her dominance, ragging on poor old me in front of... well, everybody! So there. I can't stay there any longer. I just can't!

ADAM

Really, Mother?

MOTHER

Really! What, you don't believe your own mother? I swear on my own damn grave, right up on that altar.

(pauses to scowl

What, you can't stand up for your one and only mother who gave birth to you?

ADAM
(sighing)

Don't go there, Mother. It's not that I don't believe you. I just can't believe what happened.

MOTHER

I tried to explain. If I've learned anything, it's you don't fight crazy with crazy; I was exceptionally calm. I just told her that my sweet son, who believes in reincarnation and wants my soul to be taken care of, placed me there. Must've struck a nerve.
She was all like...

(mockingly)

'I may have no children of my own, but I have Buddha in my heart, and I know you don't belong here.' Jesus Christ, the way she tried to bite my head off, you'd think I'd committed high treason!

ADAM

How petty of her.

MOTHER

Extremely petty! I put up a good fight, you know your mother can hold her own. I gotta give it to the old crone though, she has her principles. She kept talking about 'karma,' how she had earned her spot through her life's work. Yet I just took the shortcut of letting my kid pay for my place. I couldn't say anything to that. And you know what? She laughed in my face. She knew she got me. She knew those words cut deep.

ADAM

Unbelievable. Why does all that matter, in the afterlife?

MOTHER

Well sweetie, apparently it damn well matters!

(Lightning strikes and thunder booms, once again)

MOTHER

(looking up at the sky)

Alright, alright, okay kid, I really need to get a move on soon. Anyway, I need you to move me, you got that? My life down here isn't smooth sailing, thanks to...

(clears throat and continues)

somebody, and I'd like to at least be at peace now. You get that, right? I'd like the new place to be somewhere quiet, somewhere classy.

ADAM

Classy, for us living folk, equals money, dear mother.

MOTHER

Well, we all know I didn't raise you to live this life where you don't make any! Money doesn't rain from the sky and certainly isn't hiding between the pages of those damn books you can't stop reading. Get a real job!

ADAM

I think that's enough, Mother.

MOTHER

Adam Cloud, I'm asking you to listen, one last time. We only have so much time on this earth to make changes for ourselves. You may not know how precious time is now, but trust me, you'll miss it when you run out of it. Take advantage of the time you have. Make a change!

ADAM
(half-heartedly)

I'll think about it.

(Thunder roars. Lightning strikes for the last time)

MOTHER
(looks up at the thunderous sky)

Please do! Before it's too late.

(Thunder roars)

Alright, alright, I'm leaving!

(MOTHER disappears into the dark. Heavy rain starts to pour, yet ADAM still sweeps the trash, devoted to his work)

ADAM
(brushes the sweat off his brow)

Whew! How could there be so much trash? What happened on these streets today?

(ADAM continues to sweep trash into an impressive pile. As he sweeps, it almost looks like he's dancing with his broom)

ADAM

You and me, broom, my friend, we're the real thing.

(ADAM leans his broom against his cart and picks up a candle from the pile of trash)

ADAM

Just a lump of wax and a piece of string. Yet this simple creation could light the darkest room—enlighten new paths, start a revolution, begin new eras.

(He places the candle in the trash bag on his cart, turns back to the pile and picks out a piece of cloth)

ADAM

What could this gruesome little thing possibly be?

(ADAM unfolds it slowly to reveal the National Flag. He hangs the flag carefully on the cart, brushes off his collar and straightens up, to salute the flag with vigor. As the broom falls over with a thump, the flag falls to the ground. ADAM continues to scavenge through the pile of trash when plastic water bottles roll out and crash to the ground)

ADAM

All these wasted water bottles, the ultimate bottleneck, created by capitalism!

Only humans would take the most basic necessity for our survival, something Mother Earth graciously provided for free, mind you. Bottle it up, and slap a price tag on it! Shame on mankind for taking advantage of our own kind, just to make another dollar, another day. The creation of all this waste, every day. Shame on you!

ADAM rants on, steps on a black piece of trash. Similar chunks of trash can be found throughout the stage – some wrapped in newspaper like leftover food, some rolling around haphazardly, some stuck together. ADAM picks up the black chunk underfoot and examines it closely, then drops it, shrieking with fear)

ADAM

Hell! That's… a tongue! A human tongue!

(ADAM walks around the stage finding other tongues, gathering them into a pile, as he clicks his tongue)

Disgusting… revolting… rotten to the core and rock-hard. Some blood red, some black with mold, and hey, some green with envy. Why so many? Who's been tossing these around? Do some people have more than one tongue?
Don't we all?

(ADAM tosses tongues into the trash bag on his cart and moves on. Then finds office files and papers, reads each document. Drops them one by one into the cart)

ADAM

Now, what do we have here? Smells sickening. Let's see… yes, the stench of Fascism… Totalitarianism… Communism… Racism… Capitalism… these words all deserve to burn.

(shakes his head)

No weapon is more dangerous to man than one made from his own words. Somebody needs to sweep it all away before it's too late.

(ADAM stuffs the last document into the trash bag and spits on top of it, sweeps up the rest of the trash before finishing work for the day. Rain continues, thunder booms in the background, as if the skies are trying to help ADAM in his mission to clean up the city)

CURTAIN

ACT II

SCENE 1

(It is late at night, and all that can be heard is the sound of rain. To the right of the stage is ADAM's rooftop studio. There are stacks of books everywhere. ADAM sits in a chair and reads a novel. As he finishes the last page, he slowly closes the book. He flips the book and traces the spine with his fingers, then holds the book to his chest in a warm embrace)

ADAM

What a brilliant ending! What a courageous woman, with such resilience!

(Thunder booms as the rain starts to fall harder. Lightning strikes again, and HEROINE's silhouette appears outside the frosted glass door. ADAM doesn't hear her knocking, dismissing it as thunder)

ADAM

Oh, to meet such a woman in real life, to get to know such… character! I'd give anything to write like this one day. One day…

(The stranger knocks on the door, loud enough for ADAM to hear. ADAM puts the book down and checks the time. With a puzzled expression, he gets up and walks to the door)

ADAM

Who is it?

HEROINE
(from outside)

Is this 108 Utopia Avenue?

ADAM

Yes?

(ADAM opens the door. HEROINE, wet from the rain, stands outside the door, holding up a piece of paper for ADAM to see)

ADAM

I'm sorry, what is this?

HEROINE

My lease!

ADAM

For where? Here? Where I live?

HEROINE

Signed and dated, right here. As you can see, I'm moving in this month. You can call the landlord to sort it out. While you do… mind if I come in? It's raining in case you haven't noticed.

ADAM

(still confused, but remembers his manners)

Oh yes, yes, come in.

(As HEROINE enters, the dimly lit studio brightens, as if her presence alone has enlarged the space. ADAM shuts the door behind her, takes a good look at HEROINE's face)

ADAM

(gasps in surprise)

Wait… it's you! It can't be.

HEROINE

(hands her lease to ADAM, pointing at the date)

Check it yourself, if you don't believe me. I signed it last month, and the move-in date is today.

ADAM

(rubs his eyes in disbelief, stares at HEROINE, not the lease)

You really look like her!
Well, at least like what I imagined of her!

HEROINE

Excuse me?

ADAM

(coming to his senses)

Oh, sorry, it's nothing. Erm… please, sit.

(ADAM offers the chair to HEROINE who sits down. He stands behind her, pauses for a second, leans over and sniffs her hair, steps back when she notices)

ADAM

(murmuring to himself)

'She smelled like the ocean,' it read. That's a nice way to put it…

HEROINE

Come again? A nice way to put what?

(looks at the contract)

Look, the wording is very clear.

ADAM

I'm sorry? This is the first I've heard of it. I didn't agree to this… agreement!

HEROINE

Agreements, legal documents, whatever you call them, the world is run by contracts. They maintain order. They keep everything fair and square!

ADAM

Fair and square? Most contracts are ridiculously unfair.

HEROINE

Enough of this... call the landlord!

ADAM

(shakes his head)

With what? I don't have a phone.

HEROINE

Are you serious? Who doesn't have a phone? Even I have one...

(pulls her phone out of her purse)

Fine, I'll do it.

(grabs the contract off ADAM, and calls the landlord)

HEROINE

Ugh, the line is busy. Landlords! Never available when you need them.

(HEROINE tosses her phone onto a pile of books, starts to clean as if trying to create a distraction for herself. She picks up books off the floor, making neat piles in the corner, pulls out her handkerchief and starts dusting)

ADAM

Excuse me, what do you think you're doing?

HEROINE

(scans the studio for more places to clean)

Well, I can't move into this dump, can I?

ADAM

A dump?
Hands off lady, everything is right where it should be.

HEROINE

Calm down! There's nothing wrong with a little straightening up, a little order!

ADAM

These are in order! Look—this is my place, regardless of what your contract says. Common sense dictates we're not going to change anything in the middle of the night! So please, leave my things alone. Who do you think you are? A genie from a lamp? One of the shoemaker's elves? Showing up at the witching hour... like... a character in a novel.

HEROINE

(puts her hands up)

Okay, fine, fine! But you must admit, this place is a mess! I can barely find a place to put my stuff down. You don't know this, but I'm... claustrophobic. I don't need to explain myself to you but... that's just how it is.

ADAM

(mumbling to himself)

Oh, I knew that... from the book.

(HEROINE continues to tidy up. ADAM attempts to stop her but then decides to give up and picks up the book he had just finished)

ADAM

(flicks through the pages as he walks to the front of the stage)

She definitely has the same look... but something is off. The woman in the novel was quiet... submissive... she had a hint of sorrow about her... not at all like this intrusive woman. Could it be... a perversion of character? If a character leaves their environment... wait, can that even happen? Humans are everchanging, evolving... it's impossible to fully know one.

HEROINE

Pardon? Did you say something?

ADAM

Oh, n-nothing, n-never mind!

(turns back to face the audience)

It can't be though… can it?
What is real and what is fantasy?
What is happening? Is this what insanity feels like? Is it all in my head?
Am I the crazy one here?

(Agitated, ADAM shakes his head, then looks back at HEROINE, with disappointment showing on his face)

ADAM

So peculiar, so convoluted! A disarray between a person and a character. Where is the line? Was there ever a line? Between time? Between space? Between circumstance?

HEROINE
(turns towards ADAM)

Anyway. This is my place as of tomorrow!

ADAM

No way! Let's leave it at that for now. Anyway. As you can see, this place doesn't have a guest bedroom, and I'm not about to share my bed with you.

HEROINE

Well, tough break. You tell me then. Where should I go, other than my rightful house? In the pouring rain? In the middle of the night! If anyone should be leaving, it should be you!

ADAM

You can't turn up uninvited and demand to stay. That is called trespassing!

HEROINE

Trespassing?

ADAM

Yes. Trespassing! Clear as day!

(Thunder roars, as if the heavens are laughing at the irony)

HEROINE

(holds up the lease)

I'm demanding my rights, as stated here! Clear as day!

(Another clap of thunder. ADAM and HEROINE glare at each other. After a brief pause, HEROINE softens her stance, puts her hands on her hips, and stretches out her lower back)

HEROINE

You know what, I'm too tired to argue.

I've been sitting on a crowded bus, going over rough roads all day. I could really use some sleep.

ADAM

Yes, you've traveled a long way, haven't you?

HEROINE

I have.

ADAM

It really is impressive, remarkable even!
I applaud you, no I envy you for your courage to leave it all behind! That man behind!
Once an alcoholic, always an alcoholic.

HEROINE
(perks up)

I did, didn't I? I've been through it all…

(suddenly becomes very aware of where she is)

Not that you'd need to know, or even want to know.

ADAM

No, no, no, I want to, and I do know! It's all written here.

HEROINE
(raises an eyebrow)

Uh…huh. Sure.

(ADAM points to the book, that he'd placed on top of a book stack. HEROINE turns around and unzips her bag, starting to unpack)

HEROINE

(pulls out a bag of bread)

I am feeling hungry. Would you like some?

ADAM

Some bread I see… I think I can contribute to that.

(ADAM glances around. He pulls out a can of tuna from behind a book stack. HEROINE finds a newspaper in the corner and lays the pages out on the floor like a picnic blanket. ADAM pulls out some plates and utensils. They make tuna sandwiches and eat in silence)

ADAM

After Jesus was resurrected, he appeared to his disciples and shared bread and fish. Look at us with our bread and tuna. Straight out of the Bible.

HEROINE

The what?

ADAM

The Bible.

HEROINE

Hmph. Of all things, why bread and fish?

ADAM

I'm not sure. Could it be a symbol too?

HEROINE

A symbol?

ADAM

A symbol.

HEROINE

Are you a Christian?

ADAM

No, but my mother used to be.

HEROINE
(nonchalantly)

I'm not into religion and all that. Couldn't handle the guilt trips.

ADAM

I guess that's one way of looking at it.

(pause)

Hm... it has been a while since I've shared a meal with anyone at my place.

HERONE

Really! Who do you dine with?

ADAM

My books.

HEROINE

(sings quietly in a sing-song tune)

Weirdo!

ADAM

Desolate, perhaps, but I am not dissolute.

HEROINE

Anyway. I have an urgent appointment early tomorrow morning. Can I trust you to keep my bags for me?

ADAM

(nodding)

Sure, that's no problem.

HEROINE

(sighs with relief)

Thank you, and I mean that. Hey, you know what? If you don't have anywhere to go, you can crash here till you find a new place. At least for a little while.

ADAM

And tonight?

HEROINE

(yawning)

Where else would you go this late?

ADAM

(stands up, rolling his sleeves up)

I can't do much about the mess, but I can make sure you have a place to sleep tonight.

(ADAM stands up and starts stacking books in the corner as if they are bricks. He makes four small stacks, takes a piece of plywood and places it on top of the stacks, creating a makeshift bed)

ADAM

Here you go – this bed of books! It should do the trick for a night.

HEROINE

(walks around the bed, checking how sturdy it is)

Better than sleeping on stone-cold concrete.

(Heroine lies down on the bed, in a fetal position without a cover, as if planning to simply make it through the night. The lights dim as HEROINE starts to snore)

(Spotlight on ADAM shows that he is wide awake, standing by the bed, looking down at HEROINE while he compares her to the woman from his book. He holds the novel in his hands, flipping the pages, and reading every now and then)

ADAM

(ADAM mumbles to himself)

In the last chapter… ah, here... 'A new, growing heart, beating fiercely in her womb.'

(The night darkens, and rain falls harder. As the lights fade to darkness, faint sounds of a heartbeat, fast but steady, break through the soothing sound of rain on the roof)

LIGHTS OUT

SCENE 2

(Outside the door, to the left of the studio, is a cement rooftop deck. Lights fade, in the studio and on the rainy deck, rain continues, lightning strikes, flashing the silhouette of MOTHER standing in the rain)

MOTHER
(whispers)

Adam...Adam Cloud... Are you asleep?

(ADAM wakes to the sound of his mother's voice and quietly goes out the door, trying not to wake HEROINE. He closes the door behind him, standing under the awning to avoid the rain)

ADAM

Mother! I already told you that I'd think about switching temples.

MOTHER

I heard you, and that's not what I'm here for! I'm here about... that woman in there.

ADAM

Woman? Oh... her?

MOTHER

Yes, her.

ADAM

Mother, I barely know her. Nothing is going on between us.

MOTHER

I know, I know. You know she's with child, right?

ADAM

I assumed so. I read about it.

MOTHER

It can't be easy for her... You think she can handle it?

ADAM

As I said, I barely know her.

MOTHER

It's not easy you know, being a single mother. Like I was.

ADAM

Of course.

MOTHER

(gushes with pride)

You are the best thing that happened to me!

ADAM

(sheepishly)

Not this again, Mother!

MOTHER

Oh shush, it is your birthday tomorrow!

ADAM

It is? Already? Hmph, I guess I lost track of time.

MOTHER

You young people never appreciate the time you have. When will you learn? You need to get your head out of books and start paying attention to life. It wasn't easy bringing you into this life, you know!

ADAM

Of all the lives possible, why'd you bring me into this one? To this dark, hopeless world?

MOTHER

I didn't have a choice! But you do. Be strong and face this world, instead of reading about other ones that only exist on pages.

ADAM

Don't start, Mother. I'd rather get some more sleep.

MOTHER

Fine, fine, I take it back! Read your books, and of course, nurture your soul! Anyway... the real reason I'm here is…

ADAM

Just get to the point, Mother.

MOTHER

Fine, fine, so… wait, what was that noise?

ADAM

What noise?

MOTHER

You really can't hear anything?

ADAM

I hear… the rain?

MOTHER

Not that. You can't hear the voice of the little one?

ADAM

What little one?

MOTHER

I made you such beautiful ears, all for what? Closed-off and can't hear a thing. Didn't you say you were searching for something in all those pages? Seems to me, you haven't found anything yet.

ADAM

I guess your time at the temple has brought you enlightenment.

MOTHER

And meanwhile, you have sunk deeper into the abyss! Let me explain it to you in a way you'll understand. Use your imagination, like you do with all those novels!

ADAM

Fine, fine!

(ADAM and MOTHER walk closer to the studio door and lean in to listen. The sound of HEROINE softly snoring is heard. ADAM listens, then shrugs to his mom, indicating that he can't hear anything of note. He starts to walk away. MOTHER grabs him, gestures for him to listen, and repeatedly pokes him in the chest. ADAM, albeit annoyed, gives in, and leans closer to listen. A soft, glowing shade of pink lights up in the shape of a fetus. The sound of a beating heart starts to amplify but fades out as ADAM jerks his head up in surprise)

ADAM
(shocked)

Mother!

MOTHER

Oh, grow up already.

ADAM
(holds his finger up to his lips, shushing)

Shhhhh! Quiet down, before she wakes up!

MOTHER

Speak for yourself!

(ADAM nods and leans in to listen. The pink light of the fetus glows brighter)

FETUS

P-p-please… save me… please!

(ADAM jumps back, aghast)

FETUS

I... I want to live! I want to see! To feel! To know!

(ADAM looks at his mother, eyes wide open in shock. As he directs his attention to the light, MOTHER disappears into the dark)

FETUS

I crave… crave for a taste… of life!

ADAM

Is that so? I'm over it, quite frankly.

FETUS

I beg you… please… convince my mother!

ADAM

Your mother?

FETUS

Please! She's going to the doctor in the morning. She thinks it's her choice, but it's my life too! Please, convince her!

ADAM

(winces, as if he has a bitter taste in his mouth)

I'm not sure if that's something I can do...

FETUS

My heart... it's been fluttering so quickly, and oh, the rush that tingles through my veins! This is what excitement feels like, right?

ADAM

It feels like that... in the beginning. I used to feel that way once... it's been a while.

FETUS

Excited, exhilarated in anticipation! To experience the world, to have life at my fingertips!

ADAM

Sure, of course... until you look down and see your hands covered in muck. Just look at your mother. At your family!

FETUS

All I can do is listen and imagine what's happening. I want to talk to the people I love, with my voice. I want to brush away their tears, with my hands.

I want to lean my head against their chest and feel the rise and fall of every breath they take.

ADAM

Some of those breaths may be burning hot with rage. Or teeming with evil thoughts. Better steer clear before they destroy you first.

FETUS

I want to dance with the wind as my partner! Waltz through the trees in the forest, skip amongst the flowers of the field! Embrace beauty with my eyes and devour its sweet scent!

ADAM

It's not all butterflies and rainbows! More like filth and trash out here.

FETUS

Is that… the sound of rain? Oh, to feel rain against my skin! To smell dampness in the air! And… and… oh, to be alive on earth. That would be my ultimate happiness!

ADAM

You're sure you won't regret it?

FETUS

I don't care if I do! The experience alone is worth it worth everything!

ADAM

I'm not sure… if this is a place worth that much.

FETUS

I'm begging you… please! Convince my mother!

(The pink light that lights up the studio side of the stage turns off. The sound of the rain grows louder, then slowly fades out. As ADAM contemplates what just happened, MOTHER reappears behind him)

MOTHER

Son, you heard.

ADAM

W-w-what should I do?

MOTHER

You know what you're going to do. Respect the kid's wishes.

ADAM

Mother, I never knew you were pro-life.

MOTHER

I was never a conservative.

ADAM

You're not a feminist, are you?

MOTHER

Does it matter what philosophy I hold, which box I check? What matters now? There is a life to save, a life!

ADAM

Why me though? I have nothing to do with this, and I don't have any say in the matter! All I've shared with this woman, whom I just met a few hours ago, is an old can of tuna and a stale piece of bread.

Sure, none of this part has been written, but it's already happened, and I can't do anything about it!

MOTHER

Of course, you can do something about it. You are the author of your own life. You said yourself, you must take responsibility for what you can see, even when unseen by others. Remember, Adam, you too were once that child.

You were a love child out of wedlock. You too, were in danger of never being born.

ADAM

Ah, the things you choose to bring up, Mother.

MOTHER

As my belly rounded, everybody had something to say. How dare I raise you without a father? Despite it all, I brought you into the world. And you have been given a chance to help another do the same. Sure, some may call it a mistake, but creating life is no error. An entire universe needs to convene to create a single life! It is noble. It is sacred. So, help the child!

ADAM

All I can do is lend a hand till the child is born. But then what?

MOTHER

Then the answer will appear on its own, in its own time.

(MOTHER looks up at ominous black rain clouds)

Alright, alright, I'm leaving!

(Lightning strikes and thunder roars. ADAM crouches and covers his ears, MOTHER disappears from the stage)

ADAM

(rocks back and forth in a fetal position)

Help… the child… I need to help the child.

(Darkness envelopes the stage as if a wolf's jaw closes shut, and all that can be heard is the steady downpour of rain)

LIGHTS OUT

SCENE 3

(Back in the studio, Adam tosses and turns on his futon bed, trying to find sleep before daybreak. A spotlight shines on his face, highlighting his emotional turmoil. He sits up)

ADAM

Is life worth living? Or is it not...? The young
one seems to think it is. It desperately yearns
to live out the life it has barely begun.
But is this the place, to live that life?
This place, where you grind to the bone
and become a cog in the system? This world
where the one true hero is money, and
nobody is free from it?

No! No, I say! Why would one choose to live
out this scenario? Such naïveté!
A live dog is better than a dead lion, but
what power do those words hold in the pitch

dark of the jungle we live in? It's invalid and unfounded. The universe admittedly, no, undeniably, has fleeting moments of beauty.

(shakes his head)

No, no I say! It's a façade! A mirage to mask the monstrosity of the Hellhole we live in!

I've met many men going through their own version of Hell, every day. I have yet to meet a man living in his Heaven, minus the intoxicated, perhaps.

Perhaps… no, in truth… ah, yes. There are always two sides to each coin; one cannot exist without the other! We're all trapped… so, the true question is… which side would we choose? Which side should we choose?

(ADAM rolls up into a ball on the futon. The clock ticks)

After all, we are not given the choice of our prison of space or time. Even so… a goldfish can find joy in swimming circles around its glass bowl all day…yes, of course! We have the one gift that no one or nothing could take from us! That is…

(The sun rises, slowly brightening the room. HEROINE awakes, stretching as she rises from her makeshift bed of books)

ADAM

(hesitates)

What should I do? Where do I start?

HEROINE

(stretches her neck side-to-side, yawning)

Are you up?

(glances at the clock)

God, look at the time.

ADAM

You can't leave!

HEROINE

(not hearing ADAM's plea, she contemplates the leftover tuna can)

Does it still count as fasting if I just take a small bite?

ADAM

Please! You can't go there!

HEROINE

(apathetically)

Why not? Here, there, it's all the same in this crummy world.

ADAM

Show me the courage I read about;
the courage I know you have!
You've overcome it all—poverty and
exclusion, violence, and abuse... for
god's sake, you've persevered through the
unthinkable!

HEROINE

You may be book-smart, but you know nothing. It's not easy, living with a man like that. My reality is as complex as an intricate fantasy, and you don't know the half of it. Life is hard!

ADAM

It's the same for me as well!

HEROINE

Above all, it isn't right to invite another person to this pity party.

ADAM

The new life deserves an invite, regardless of your views. Give it time! It wants to see the world, to feel it, know it—to touch it! All it wants to do is... exist! Who are we to deny it the chance to live a life? Trust me, I'm the last person to vouch for this life.

I thought about it all night, and took a long hard look at myself. So… please!

(HERONE looks down at her shoes)

ADAM

Give the child a chance! The gift of time!

HEROINE

Speaking of time, I need to leave. I'm going to be late.

(HEROINE gathers her things and hurries out of the room. ADAM pauses, stunned, then shakes his head and follows her out the door, but he is too late. In her place, MOTHER stands on the rooftop deck, with a solemn expression)

ADAM

Mother… what can I do? I should have talked her out of it... I should have been a little more persuasive... I...

MOTHER

You did what you could. She's only human, she'll come around.

ADAM

Will she?

MOTHER

If it's the right thing to do, she'll come around. She will indeed.

(changing attitude)

But then again. People don't change, they really don't. You'd think a matter of life and death would, but hell no, people take their pigheadedness to the grave! Like that old hag! Now, that wench has turned the other spirits against me, and they're ganging up on me now.

ADAM

How petty.

MOTHER

The pettiest! Oh, she is simply the worst. I tried to keep my head down, but I couldn't take it anymore. I stood up for myself! I told them! How they should be ashamed to act in the name of religion. The heavens know no borders, no class, no race!

ADAM

Bigotry in the afterlife? Surprising.

MOTHER

Oh, you don't know the half of it. The afterlife is just an extension of this life.

Thanks to the old hag and her hissy fit, the entire temple has been abuzz. Silent ceremony service is now heated up to full-blown debates, and sides are being taken. Everything is so… political.

There are three main parties in the temple: the original Buddhists, the ones with Buddhist children, and the rest. I'm in the rare group of Christians. I'm in the… everlasting minority, you'd say.

ADAM

Don't let it get to you. It doesn't mean anything!

MOTHER

I hear you! And I'm going to stand my ground. I wanted to tell you that there's no need to worry about moving me. What's the point of a classier temple? Heaven is where I'm standing.

ADAM

I see your vigor remains vigilant!

MOTHER

That it does! So, forget what I said before. Don't worry about making money and all that. Disregard everything!

(looks up at the sky)

Alright, alright, I'm leaving!

(MOTHER looks fondly at ADAM and disappears into the dark)

(ADAM stands in her place, sighing. Suddenly, he remembers something and walks back into the studio. He picks up the novel, flicking through the pages)

ADAM

Perhaps...?

(loud knocking on the door)

BOYFRIEND

Anybody home?

ADAM

Who is it?

(ADAM clutches the novel with his hands and slowly opens the door, turning towards the rooftop deck. BOYFRIEND stands there, wearing a wet black raincoat, the hood covering his head. His back is hunched over)

ADAM

(mumbles to himself)

Is he... a hunchback? Or... is he carrying a child under that raincoat?

BOYFRIEND

(looks at a piece of paper)

Is this… 108 Utopia Avenue?

ADAM

I believe so…?

(Before ADAM can finish, BOYFRIEND throws his raincoat on the ground and charges at ADAM, rolling up his sleeves. Under his raincoat, he has a guitar bag strapped onto him)

BOYFRIEND

Where is she?

ADAM

Who?

BOYFRIEND

Don't try and be smart, I know she's here!

ADAM

What!

BOYFRIEND

Don't play games with me now!

ADAM

Time out, time out! Look! This is my place.

You're trespassing.

(BOYFRIEND pauses for a second, blows the hair out of his eyes, and pauses to look around. He discovers the bed made of books in the corner)

BOYFRIEND
(points at the bed)

Well, well, well… what do we have here?
I see what's been going on…

ADAM

Oh no, no, no…it's just a bed made of books.

BOYFRIEND

Might as well be made of hay for you two to roll around in!

(BOYFRIEND rolls up his sleeves)

Oh, you're going to get it now… you're more devious than you look. Do you want a taste of my fist?

ADAM

Hey! You're not listening!

BOYFRIEND
(grabs ADAM by the collar)

You want me to listen? Then speak the truth, boy.

ADAM

Whoa, whoa, for goodness sake! The truth! It… isn't like that.

BOYFRIEND

Look here, skinny boy! All I hear is a bunch of lies blowing out of your ass!

ADAM

Well, that's a low blow. If you're so strong and built, why are you leeching off a woman?

BOYFRIEND

What the… what'd you call me… a leech? And who am I living off? You don't know jack shite, boy! Raving on, when you know nothing about art. You think art can be achieved without sacrifice? Without a price? You call me a leech, sucking on the blood of others? Well, I'll tell you what boy, I too bleed. I bleed a lot.

(ADAM manages to break free from BOYFRIEND's grasp and escapes to the rooftop deck. BOYFRIEND lunges at him. After a few laps around the deck, BOYFRIEND tackles ADAM and drags him towards the middle of the stage)

BOYFRIEND

(holds up a fist)

Oh, you're going to get it now.

ADAM

You really are, as you were in the book!
Although, you seem... much worse.

BOYFRIEND

Stop raving before I shut you up for good!

(As BOYFRIEND lifts his fist about to strike, HEROINE enters. She walks slowly, with her head down)

BOYFRIEND

Well, well, well... what have we here.
Get your ass over here!

(BOYFRIEND shouts at HEROINE. HEROINE stares at him, then walks away into the studio, her head held high)

BOYFRIEND

Oh, is that how we're playing it now?

ADAM

(tries to free himself from BOYFRIEND's grasp, ADAM calls out to HEROINE)

A-a-are you okay?

(HEROINE doesn't reply. BOYFRIEND and ADAM look at each other, and with curious expressions, stop fighting and follow HEROINE into the studio. HEROINE sits on the bed made of books. The three stand still, as if in a stop motion film)

HEROINE

Could I bother you for some water?

ADAM

Yes, yes, water, of course.

(ADAM brings out a gallon-size water bottle. He lugs it over and drops it next to HEROINE. Next to her, the bottle looks comically large. She opens a packet of prescription pills, lifts the bottle with ease, and swallows them)

ADAM

So… that's it? Is that it for the child?

(HEROINE looks ADAM in the eye, then hesitates. She looks down at her empty pill packet, then shakes her head with regret. Silence sweeps through the studio)

HEROINE

(shakes her head harder)

I… I… I just couldn't. I was ready… I even got on the table… but right as they were about to numb me, I stopped. I couldn't bear the thought of it.

ADAM

(elated)

Good! Good for you!

(BOYFRIEND looks back and forth, between the two, trying to put the pieces together)

BOYFRIEND

What child? Christ! What is happening here?

ADAM

Must I spell it out for you? It's your baby! Your child will get a chance to be born into this world!

BOYFRIEND

(stares at her in disbelief)

Is it true...?

(HEROINE sits in silence)

ADAM

You call yourself an artist, yet you are blind to what's happening right in front of you.

BOYFRIEND

I'm asking you again... Is... it... true?

(HEROINE continues to stay silent)

ADAM

How can you create music for the soul, when you don't pay attention to the souls around you? Art comes from your reality, not from the bottom of a bottle! How can you sing of the delicacies of human emotion, when you smash it down with your fist?

(BOYFRIEND looks down at the floor with a solemn face, gripping his guitar bag. He slowly sits down to open the guitar bag. He finds his cigarette packet inside. As he grabs it, he pulls a guitar string by mistake. A lone note reverberates through the studio with a twang. He puts the cigarette in his mouth but then throws it on the ground, before lighting it)

BOYFRIEND

You didn't think twice about mentioning it to me?

(HEROINE maintains her silence)

BOYFRIEND

Babe, I can explain…

(HEROINE doesn't respond)

BOYFRIEND

It was the alcohol! Are you even listening?

(HEROINE sits still, without blinking)

BOYFRIEND

Forgive me, I'm begging you.

I'll stop drinking, I swear!

ADAM
(scoffs)

As if!

BOYFRIEND

From now on, I'm focusing on my music... and you. Nothing else.

ADAM

Ha! Lies.

BOYFRIEND
(glares)

Shut it! You don't know a damn thing.

ADAM

Well, according to the book... never mind... I just know, okay?

BOYFRIEND
(turns back to HEROINE)

Babe… sugar doll, please. Believe me.

(HEROINE stays silent)

ADAM

Don't trust a word from that drunkard! Once an alcoholic, always an alcoholic.

BOYFRIEND
(growls at ADAM)

Didn't I tell you to shut it?
Who do you think you are, her little brother?
That's it…

(BOYFRIEND charges at ADAM and grabs him by the collar again)

ADAM

Oh, is this what you're promising her?
Use your brain, Neanderthal!

HEROINE

Leave him alone!

BOYFRIEND

This fool's gotta learn to keep his nose out of other people's business!

(ADAM gasps for air as BOYFRIEND's tightens his grip)

HEROINE

How do you expect me to forgive you?
What is going to change?

BOYFRIEND
(taken aback)

Well… it is…

HERONE

Every time! All you do is talk and talk!
But I don't see you walk the talk.
Where is this change you're talking about?

BOYFRIEND

(still holding ADAM in his grip)

Well... you know... hm...

HEROINE

I've supported us through our whole relationship. When did you bring home a dime, even when you were getting paid for your gigs at the club?

BOYFRIEND

Well... that was...

ADAM

I need some air! Can you let go of me first, and then have this conversation?

HEROINE

You swore to go sober, every time. Yet, I still see you drinking, every day.

BOYFRIEND

Erm... well...

ADAM

(struggles to break free)

Erm… well…

HEROINE

I supported your dreams!
I'd save up to buy you your precious guitars.
All for you to get drunk and smash them into pieces!

BOYFRIEND

I did? Did I…?

HEROINE

You'd say you need inspiration for your work. Then you'd waste your days chasing inspiration in bars and clubs, who knows where. All while I worked to the bone in the factory, to feed you, and your inspiration!

BOYFRIEND

What can I say—that I'm sorry?

HEROINE

I don't deserve this. I can't live like this!

(HEROINE breaks into tears, sobbing as she remembers the pains of the past. BOYFRIEND panics, letting go of ADAM, and rushes over to HEROINE. ADAM falls backwards, hitting his head on a book pile)

ADAM

Ouch! Ow!

HEROINE

Are you alright? It looked like you hit your head pretty hard!

BOYFRIEND

Sorry about that. Are… you okay?

ADAM

(ADAM slowly gets up, rubbing his head)

It's your lucky day, I'm not dead yet!

HEROINE

Whew, that's a relief.

BOYFRIEND

It's like you're made of paper.

ADAM

(taken aback, starts hiccupping)

Hic! This part-hic! wasn't in the-hic! story. Why am I-hic! the one-hic! getting hurt?

HEROINE

(looks at BOYFRIEND)

Can you do something?

BOYFRIEND

Come here, let me help you.

ADAM

(waves BOYFRIEND away)

It's-hic!-okay, I'll be-hic! fine.

BOYFRIEND

I said, come here! I can make it stop!

ADAM

(continues to wave BOYFRIEND away)

It's fine–hic!–I'm telling–hic!–you–hic! It's fine!–hic!

BOYFRIEND

Well, it's not fine for me. I've got sensitive ears! Your hiccups are off rhythm and it's bugging the hell out of me! Come here!

ADAM

(mumbles to himself)

This is weird. This is so… out of character for him. Is the novel asking me to steer the ending towards someplace else?

(BOYFRIEND grabs hold of ADAM and massages pressure points on his back. ADAM's hiccups stop)

ADAM

Oh whoa, that worked! No more hiccups!

BOYFRIEND

I got a trick or two up my sleeve. I dabbled in acupressure back in the day.

ADAM
(mumbles)

Hmm, that wasn't in the novel either.

BOYFRIEND

I could be a decent man if it weren't for the booze.

ADAM
(mumbles)

Perhaps reality is much more intricate, an endless array of knowledge beyond what's necessary to comprehend the story's plotline.

(BOYFRIEND kneels before HEROINE, speaks lovingly, in a sing-song voice)

BOYFRIEND

Babe... Give us another chance... I'm nothing without you, just a wreck. You've been gone for a day and it's like the sun has disappeared. You're the reason why I've been holding on this long. I can do better. I can make this work, I promise, my love!

HEROINE
(expression softens)

Promise me that you'll lay off the bottle.

BOYFRIEND

You have my word.

HEROINE

That you'll prioritize health and stability.

BOYFRIEND

I will.

ADAM

You better.

HEROINE

Promise to never crush my soul… or yours.

BOYFRIEND

I promise… I'll give it my all, all for you, honey. Speaking of things for you… I wrote you a song. I'd like to play it for you… if that's okay.

BOYFRIEND

(opens the guitar case)

Is that okay?

ADAM

(butting in)

I'd like to hear.

HEROINE

(rubbing her stomach)

Sure… the baby seems to want to hear it too.

ADAM

I read that your voice was a gift from the gods. That you could sing like the flow of the river. When you play, the stars in the sky swoon and descend from the heavens, twinkling in our world. So please play! Play for us and your child!

BOYFRIEND

(smiles sheepishly)

Um… ok. Well, then…

(BOYFRIEND plucks a few guitar strings with his long, dirty fingernails, tuning his guitar. He closes his eyes and begins to play. A soft, sad tune fills the studio)

THE VOYAGER SONG

O, hold my hand and stand with me
So we can be a vast sea
Over the rolling waves we wade
Over the days we crusade
I ran by the river blind
Ran by the ocean blind
I'm nothing but a shipwreck
Scattered fragments of my mind
O, hold my hand and stand with me
So we can be a vast sea
Over the harsh wind of the storm
Into the night, be reborn
Ah ha, ah ha, I am nothing but a shipwreck.

ADAM
(stands up, applauding)

Oh, I'm just speechless!

HEROINE

It's a beautiful song.

ADAM

When you get your act together, someday soon, you'll be a shining star!

BOYFRIEND

I guess I have a new fan now. Well… thanks.

(ADAM faces the audience and walks towards the center of the stage. As he begins to speak, HEROINE and BOYFRIEND freeze like statues, emphasizing that ADAM is now the narrator of this novel, and the couple are the main characters)

ADAM

What a surprise! Such a poor character, yet he sings with real grace! Life never ceases to astonish! And that word, love. That four-lettered word! You'd think it's foolish, childish, useless. But it's magical!

Like a tiny cube of sugar melting into the darkness of a cup of coffee, to transform utter bitterness into something sweet. Those four letters put together calmed down the tornado of events. It's a wonder!

Love, music—from which world is such beauty created?

(ADAM stops to think. HEROINE and BOYFRIEND unfreeze, then start to pick up their belongings)

BOYFRIEND

Babe, we've got to hurry if we're going to catch the last train.

HEROINE

Yes, let's.

(turns to ADAM)

Thank you. I only spent one night with you but it felt like a thousand nights.

ADAM

I feel the same!

HEROINE

Maybe it's time to put down those books and look for somebody out there.

ADAM

Mm, I'm going to have to look for a job first.

HEROINE

Love always comes first.

BOYFRIEND

(holds his hand out to shake ADAM's)

You know what? I just realized I don't even know your name!

ADAM

(shakes BOYFRIEND's hand firmly)

Adam, Adam Cloud.

BOYFRIEND

Call me Malik. It's a stage name, for now. Means Ocean, or King.

HEROINE

And my name is…

ADAM

I know. It's in the book.

HEROINE
(taken aback)

You keep mentioning some book... you sure you're okay? You seem… light-headed. Oh, and I apologize for Malik.

BOYFRIEND

It's not my fault this guy speaks nonsense.

ADAM

Well, actually…

HEROINE

Adam, your youth won't last forever! You got to make sure you eat properly, even if you're alone.

ADAM

Don't worry about me. Things are going to change! For all of us!

HEROINE

You think so?

ADAM

I believe so.

HEROINE

Won't the past repeat?

ADAM

It might.

(BOYFRIEND shakes his head)

HEROINE
(furrows her brow)

And if it does?

ADAM

Even if it does. Things will be different. There will be a new life in the mix. And Mr. Malik here... well, beautiful songs come from beautiful people.

HEROINE

And I can put my faith in that?

BOYFRIEND

Babe, believe me!

ADAM

Believing is all we can do, and all we shall do. The gift of art will change him, no, it will change all of us! And more than anything… we still have time.

HEROINE

You're right about that, we have all been given the gift of time!

ADAM

Yes, we need to live that time well.

BOYFRIEND
(holding HEROINE's hand)

I'll try hard to make the most of time.

HEROINE

I wish you well Adam!

ADAM

And I wish you the same.

(BOYFRIEND starts to walk out the door. HEROINE follows him)

BOYFRIEND

We better get a move on.

HEROINE

Yes, no time to waste. Goodbye Adam, and thank you.

(HEROINE and BOYFRIEND carry their bags out. Right before they exit, they freeze like statues. A soft, glowing shade of pink lights up behind her, in the shape of a fetus. The delicate, yet excited voice of the new life echoes across the stage)

FETUS

Thank you!

ADAM

(smiles, and mumbles to himself)

You're welcome… and take care of those two.

(Stage lights slowly fade out, until only a spotlight shines on ADAM)

LIGHTS OUT

EPILOGUE

(As the spotlight on ADAM slowly widens and the lights across the stage fade in, ADAM finds himself back in his studio, alone. The bed made of books is gone, and everything is the way it was before HEROINE's arrival. He picks up the novel that he had just finished the day before. It is drenched in water as if it had been left outside in the rain)

ADAM

Oh dear, it's completely soaked!
Every single page is drenched.

(He carefully lifts the book and places it on the bookshelf, so nothing gets torn. He brings his hand to his chest and bows politely, as if he is sending a prayer to his ancestors. He finds another book from the shelf and slowly opens the first page)

ADAM

A dream dreamed alone is simply unfinished
A dream dreamed together?
Now that's something special.
Someday, someone will come knocking
on that door and make an entrance into
my story. Till then...

(ADAM pulls out a candle from a drawer and places it on a bookshelf. He lights it with a match. He glances at the novel he had just put aside and whispers)

ADAM

Happy birthday to you, who is also me.
Happy birthday to you, who is also me.

(As ADAM blows out the candle, the lights turn off, and the sound of pouring rain fills the theatre)

LIGHTS OUT & CURTAIN

And if he left off dreaming about you...

—Lewis Carroll

CLONE 1001

THE PLAYERS

ART
19-year-old male. Product of human cloning project. He is a spitting image of MR OH; how the back of his hair spikes up like an antenna

FATHER
ART's father. A simple country man who works as a security guard at the BioTech company

MOTHER
ART's mother. A practical woman with a loud voice

STELLA
ART's girlfriend

DR. HA
Vice President of BioTech company

MR. OH
Genetic source of ART. Chairman of BioTech company He looks like an older version of ART; how the back of his hair spikes up like an antenna

LORD
Leader of the anti-human cloning movement

RIGHT HAND & LEFT HAND
Followers of LORD

MAGICIAN
Mysterious man wearing a top hat with white gloves

MAGICIAN'S REFLECTION
Reminds the MAGICIAN 'to thine own self be true'

THE SCENE

Large mirrors stand parallel to one another on each side of the stage, angled to create the Droste Effect, to show an infinite number of reflections when characters stand on stage.

PROLOGUE

The curtain rises in complete darkness. Slowly, a jazzy tune starts to ramp up, as if a jack-in-the-box toy is being wound up. As the tune comes to a crescendo, a single spotlight switches on, showing MAGICIAN standing, as though he has magically appeared. The audience can see an array of reflections of MAGICIAN from mirrors positioned house left and house right.

MAGICIAN bows towards the audience, then pulls a conductor's baton from the inside pocket of his jacket. He swivels slowly, turning his back to the audience. As he lifts his arms like a conductor, a projector starts displaying images on the back wall of the stage.

Using conductor's movements, MAGICIAN tells the tale of the creation of the universe. He starts with the Big Bang, as stars explode on the screen like fireworks. He pulls the pieces together to create a galaxy, then piles up sparkles to create the sun. He pulls some pieces apart, shaping them like clay, to create the moon.

Then using his baton like a pen, he draws constellations. As his movements get more exaggerated, and the music grows louder, a large blue planet emerges on the stage. MAGICIAN raises his arms, as if he is lifting Earth into the sky, then glances back towards the audience. The music stops. MAGICIAN pauses, making eye contact with the audience. He slowly lifts his finger for dramatic effect, then points at the blue Earth.

MAGICIAN

This… is where we are.

(MAGICIAN slowly takes a few steps towards Earth. He holds his hand up, blowing on it to create a gust of wind. Trees and grass sprout on Earth. He waves his arms like a conductor, then with a smile and a wink, conjures up a single flower onto his white gloved hand)

MAGICIAN

Stunning… is it not?

(MAGICIAN lifts his arms, conjures up a white dove and releases it to fly away)

MAGICIAN

(blows a kiss towards the dove)

Liberating… is it not?

*(MAGICIAN takes a deep breath, raises one arm and pulls a puppy from his jacket. The puppy whimpers and starts to bark incessantly. MAGICIAN cuddles the puppy but grimaces when it begins to yelp and drops the puppy. *For the dove and puppy, no real animals shall be used but implied through sound or visual effect)*

MAGICIAN

Silence, mutt!

(MAGICIAN, wary of the audience, clears his throat and straightens his collar. Waves a hand and wipes away the sun, the moon, and the galaxy)

(Lights dim. MAGICIAN turns to face the audience. A harp dramatically strikes a chord, trees start to sprout behind him, branching out to create striking visual patterns. Leaves and blossoms emerge on growing branches, attracting a kaleidoscope of red butterflies. They swarm around the MAGICIAN's heart)

MAGICIAN

Nature never repeats itself. Never! Ever!

(MAGICIAN turns his back to the audience; starts to mold something out of thin air as if he is at a pottery wheel. He is

meticulous, building up and then crushing his work repeatedly, aiming for perfection. He wipes the sweat from his brow. Finally satisfied, he carefully places his masterpiece onto his palm. It is a human being)

MAGICIAN
(inspects the human in his palm, mumbles to himself then speaks threateningly)

Well… this one's going to cause a headache, will it not?

(MAGICIAN'S REFLECTION grows bigger. It suddenly jumps out of the mirror and looks around in awe)

MAGICIAN

Wow…oh wooow…Who…what are you?

(MAGICIAN'S REFLECTION examines the world around him, like a newborn baby. MAGICIAN stands up, brushing himself off)

MAGICIAN

Do you… speak?

MAGICIAN'S REFLECTION
(nods)

MAGICIAN

Speak, then! Who are you, and where do you come from?

MAGICIAN'S REFLECTION

(mocks in response)

Who are you? Where do you come from?

MAGICIAN

(stunned by this unexpected, disrespectful answer)

Well… ah… well, I… am me, myself, I mean, I am the creator. You… well I created you.

MAGICIAN'S REFLECTION

You think? You really think it's going to work? Your creation of me?

(MAGICIAN'S REFLECTION lifts his hand and makes a finger gun. He points his finger gun towards Magician and shoots. MAGICIAN falls back, clutching his heart. He looks at MAGICIAN'S REFLECTION, then back at his hand clutching his heart, in complete disbelief)

MAGICIAN

(crys out in pain)

Who… what? H-h-how…. could this be happening?

(MAGICIAN slowly dies. MAGICIAN'S REFLECTION blows imaginary smoke from the end of his finger gun. He lowers his hand, looks towards the audience and shrugs)

MAGICIAN'S REFLECTION

Seems like you don't have all the answers, Mr. Creator! Answer me this: what sort of divinity could be vanquished with a few words, from none other than… me?

(MAGICIAN'S REFLECTION walks up to the body and pokes it with his foot a few times to check if it's alive or dead. MAGICIAN'S REFLECTION grunts, lifts the limp body, slings it over his shoulder and exits into the dark)

LIGHTS OUT

SCENE 1

(The sun sets across the riverbank of the Korean countryside. The rhythmic noise of a knife chopping can be heard from the kitchen, as dinner is being prepared. The sound of footsteps, pacing back and forth on the front porch can be heard, along with the mumbling of Father's voice. He mumbles repeatedly, trying out different intonations and voices, as he walks to the rhythm of the kitchen sounds)

FATHER

Who are you? Ahem, no, who are you? Who are you? I am a father. I am a father. I am a father!

(Father enters through the front door with his nose in an English language textbook. As he walks in through the door, he looks up, notices MOTHER cooking in the kitchen, and swerves in her direction. Completely immersed in her cooking, she doesn't look up)

FATHER

(points at her, and speaks in an awkward American accent)

Who... are... you?

(Without waiting for MOTHER's reply, he answers himself, as if he were in a one-man play. His intonation and pronunciation are awkward, as he tries to cover up his foreign accent)

FATHER

I... am... a... mother. I am a mother.

MOTHER

(annoyed, points the kitchen knife towards the door)

Oh, stop it with that nonsense. I don't need that American lingo in my kitchen!

(FATHER grins sheepishly and scoots out of the kitchen towards East. He finds ART in a headstand. FATHER walks up to his upside-down son and reads from his English textbook)

FATHER

(pointing at ART)

Who... are... you?

FATHER

(he answers himself, as if trying to memorize the answer)

I... am... a... son. I am a son.

ART

(red-faced from being upside down)

Not now, Pops. I'm trying to clear my head of the nightmare I had last night. My dream was a terrifying purification!

FATHER

You can purify your dream? Is such a thing possible?

ART

Of course it's not, but it's all I can do for now. I just can't seem to shake it off, some of those images were horrifying. I'm hoping this will help somehow.

FATHER

Whatever keeps you busy, Arty Boy. I'll leave you to it.

(He holds his book up and pauses for a second. Then he walks towards the South, standing at the front of the stage, looking out at the audience. He shrugs. Hesitating for a moment, he points at the audience)

FATHER

Who... are... you? Why... you... here?

ART

(coming back down onto his feet, agitated)

Pops, that's just wrong.

FATHER

Oh, what now? What's wrong?

ART

(walks up to FATHER, looks at his book)

Asking somebody who they are, that's just redundant. And rude, to think of it. You can see who they are, can't you?

FATHER

You'd be surprised, boy. You can't always believe what you see. Never hurts to ask. How about you try?

ART

Fine. Look, it's all in the tone, the intonation. Nobody will get what you're saying if you're not emphasizing the right word. When you ask somebody who they are, you put the emphasis on the 'who' and end it by raising the last word 'you'. Like this: 'Who are you?'

(ART and FATHER face each other, repeating back and forth (using varied word stress) the phrase "who are you?". The amount of effort they put into it, especially FATHER, is comical)

FATHER

WHO! WHO! WHEW are you?

ART

No, not 'Whew', 'Who'! WHO are you?

FATHER

I... am... a... father! WHEW! Are youuuu?

ART

(almost singing)

I am a son! I am a son!

MOTHER

(shakes the kitchen knife in the air)

You better quit that before I come out and show you who the hell I am. Now calm down and make yourselves useful by peeling some garlic.

(The family is interrupted by the sound of the doorbell. ART's face lights up, as he hurries to the door and opens it. STELLA enters, wearing a very short floral mini skirt)

FATHER

(trys out one of the new phrases he used with ART)

WHEW are youuuu?

ART

(embarrassed)

Pops, stop it.
You know Stella—she's my girl!

STELLA

(plays along)

I... am... his... girlfriend.

(STELLA curtsies to FATHER with a wink, then presents Art with red flowers. The flowers have the same pattern as her skirt, creating the illusion that she pulled them out from under her skirt)

STELLA

Happy birthday, Arty sweetheart!

ART

(accepts the flowers)

Aw, thanks doll.

(ART gives STELLA a hug, which turns into a prolonged embrace. MOTHER watches and frowns)

MOTHER

Hey, hey, enough already.

FATHER

(changes the subject)

Big day for my big son!
All grown up and ready to see the world. It's going to be hard, living amongst foreigners, speaking a foreign language.

MOTHER

Nonsense, worry about yourself! Your tongue is going to get cramps the way you've been practicing gibberish.

STELLA

I think it's perfectly respectable.
Learning new things is hard at his age!

MOTHER

Oh, butt out of it.

STELLA

English is the world's language!
To speak it is to speak words of global success!

MOTHER

The world's language? Ha! There's more to Earth than America! Learn to love your mother tongue, I say.

STELLA

Speaking English opens doors.
Like jobs.
Like degrees.
Like opportunities!

MOTHER

(shakes her head in resignation)

Fine, fine, it's not like any of you listen to me anyway.

FATHER

Stella is right. She's got a point.
In this day and age, we need to learn English as well. Why, just look at the signs on the streets. We should at least be able to read the names of the new stores in town, shouldn't we?

(opens his book again)

WHEW... are youuuu?
I... am a... FATHER.
WHEW... are youuuu?
I! Am a Mother!

(MOTHER shakes her head, glares at her husband for a second, then yells)

MOTHER

Are you going to help me peel this garlic or what? Art, boy, don't just stand there, your bags aren't going to pack themselves!

FATHER

Yes ma'am.

(FATHER salutes MOTHER and promptly heads to the kitchen. ART takes STELLA's hand and sneaks away to his room. He stops, as he remembers his nightmare from the previous night)

ART

I've seen this image before... yep... it's déjà vu! It was the four of us, just like this.
I was...

(shudders)

murdered.

FATHER

What a nightmare!

ART

Horrifying!

MOTHER

Well, who did it? Who would murder you?

ART

I'd rather not say…

STELLA

It's just a dream, babe. So, tell us what happened! Who would dare murder my big strong man?

ART

It was… all of you!

FATHER, MOTHER, STELLA

(in unison)

We did what?

ART

Yes, Mom, Pops, even you Stella! The three of you pushed me off a cliff. There was an audience even! The whole crowd watched as I was falling to my death. As if I was some circus act! They even cheered. Chills me to the bone just thinking about it.

MOTHER

What a bizarre dream. You and your odd imagination are working overtime, even in your sleep.

FATHER

Even if it was just a dream, I'm sorry.

MOTHER
(agitated)

Now why would you be sorry, when you said so yourself that it's just a dream?

(shakes her head)

Art, didn't I tell you to go pack your bags?

ART

Now why are you getting all worked up?

MOTHER

It's just bad luck, dreaming about dying. Especially on your birthday.

STELLA

Hmmm. Interesting how your family is always finding something to bicker about when you're just three people. My place is a full house, with my folks, grandparents, cousins, uncles, and aunts... but you'd never hear us fighting.

MOTHER
(sarcastically)

Well, isn't that nice. Must be since everybody is busy with the diner.

STELLA

Ahem, it's a restaurant, not a diner.

MOTHER

Oh, my apologies, I didn't know your fine establishment was now serving the queen! A restaurant, ha! Is that what we're calling mom-and-pop diners now? And besides, if your family is so peaceful and happy, why are you spending night after night in this madhouse?

STELLA

Well, every house has a rebel, an outcast, a black sheep. Had my folks just accepted me for who I was.

MOTHER

And who is that exactly?

ART

Mom, why can't you be nicer to Stella?

MOTHER

Doesn't get any sweeter than that, son.

(FATHER steps in between the quarrel blowing a whistle, holding his arms out like a sports referee in action. He is still holding his textbook in one hand)

FATHER

Enough!

MOTHER

Hey! What are you doing exactly, and where did you get that whistle? What are you now, a family referee?

FATHER

Enough! Today is a good day. Our boy turns twenty! And on top of that, he heads off to college tomorrow. We don't have the time for nonsense—let's just be happy!

MOTHER

(heads back to the kitchen counter)

Well, why do you think I've been slaving all day?

(shaking her head)

The nerve! To tell me off when you haven't lifted a single finger to help.

FATHER

(turns to ART)

Son, I think I told you before, but we have some important guests coming for your birthday dinner. Including people from BioTech!

ART

Dr. Ha is coming?

FATHER

The very man himself. The man behind the curtain, your benefactor!

MOTHER

No need to get too excited, now.
Anyway, didn't you say you'd tell him?

FATHER

Ahem... well... I did...

MOTHER

Tell him already. You're the one who started it.

ART

Tell me what?

FATHER

(avoiding eye contact with ART)

That... is... well... son...

ART

I'm listening. What is it?

FATHER

Hmm… well… maybe now is not the time for this. Maybe later…

MOTHER

You make my blood boil over.

(groans)

You're going to be the death of me!

FATHER

Now, let's not get extreme here…

ART

Pops, what's going on?

FATHER

Don't mind her. Are you done packing?

ART

Almost...

(looks back at STELLA)

C'mon, let's go to my room.

STELLA

Okay. It's not like I have anything going on here.

MOTHER
(looks offended)

Does anybody listen to what I say?
Besides, what urgent business have you got in there every day, behind closed doors?
Let me guess!

ART
(winks)

You'd know, Ma. You must've been young once.

MOTHER
(blushing)

I have no idea what you're talking about.

FATHER
(grinning)

Oh, I remember.

MOTHER
(holds up the kitchen knife)

Let's just leave it at that, shall we?

(ART and STELLA go into ART's room. From this point, the lights switch back and forth between (A) the kitchen and (B) ART's room. Lights switch on at (B) ART's room. ART takes STELLA's hand and leads her to the windowsill. They sit together with his arms around her, lovingly)

STELLA

(sarcastically)

Can't wait for her to be my mother-in-law one day.

ART

Aw, you know she loves you to bits.

STELLA

Ha! Still…

ART

What?

STELLA

You know… she's always so… pointed. Just looking to find something wrong.

(ART shakes his head with a smile)

STELLA

Are you sure she's not your stepmom?

ART

(changes the subject)

Enough of that nonsense, look here, doll. Not over there, here, eyes on me.

STELLA
(turns to look him in the eye)

On you?

ART

That's right, on me. You know... we're not going to see each other for a while.

STELLA
(looks into ART's eyes, and looks down at his lips)

Mmhmm, and...?

ART
(draws her closer)

Mmhmm, so...

(ART and STELLA lean into each other for a kiss. Suddenly, glass shatters in the kitchen and MOTHER screams. ART and STELLA freeze, surprised. Lights out)

(Lights switch on in (A) the kitchen and den area. FATHER stands still, gripping onto the tilted table, his eyes wide open in shock. He has just walked into the table, causing everything to crash onto the ground, including a large serving plate of fish. The plate has shattered, and the whole fish is on the floor. MOTHER is right behind him, her hands covering her mouth as she screams)

MOTHER

(drops to her hands and knees and scoops up the fish)

Gosh darn it—not the perch!

FATHER

(shakes his head)

Not the perch! I was out early for that one, all for our boy's special dinner!

MOTHER

(sits back in resignation)

What a waste. I'm exhausted. Exhausted by everything!

(looks up at Father)

What are we going to do when the boy is gone? What are we going to do for money?

FATHER

Well… I've still got the security guard job at the lab.

MOTHER

That's nothing! Doesn't even pay the mortgage!

FATHER

We never have problems for long, we'll be fine.

(Lights switch to (B) ART's room. ART and STELLA are holding hands)

ART

Sometimes… I just don't know who I am.

STELLA

We all think that.

ART

You know what I mean. I'm just… different. I'm not at all like my folks. I don't look like them, I certainly don't think like them. Sure, Pops is the best, but I just feel like something is missing. That something… is wrong. With me.

STELLA

Now why would you think that?

ART

No reason. It's just how I feel. I feel… all alone, more often than not. I haven't told this to anyone… but yesterday's nightmare wasn't a first. It happens every night.

STELLA

Dreams are just dreams. Simple as that.

ART

Maybe. Or maybe not. In my dreams, this... man follows me around. An old fogey with a weird cane. He just follows me around, like a shadow. As if... he's a part of me. Like a different side of me. Like I created him and can't get rid of him. It's too... confusing. Babe, you're the only one I've told this to.

STELLA

That is... an interesting dream to have. Over and over, too.

(pauses in thought)

Could it be... God?

ART

Seems like a stretch.

STELLA

You said he's strict. He's stern. And he judges. Sounds like God to me.

ART

(thinks for a second, then shakes his head)

It can't be. The image is too... specific for it to be God. I'm pretty sure God isn't walking around with a cane.

STELLA

(leaning in and changing her tone suggestively)

Well... let's just forget about that for now... at least for today...

ART

(noticing Stella's advances, leans in)

Oh, ok... yea... never mind all that...

STELLA

I'll always wait for you, even when you're gone. Just like that moon in the sky.

ART

Girl, you're my star. Don't you dare be like the moon. That fickle moon changes every day.

STELLA

(laughs)

If you say so. Well... the sun is technically a star, right? I'll shine, not burn, every day waiting for you.

(ART and STELLA lean in for a kiss. Once again, they are interrupted by a loud crashing noise and MOTHER screaming. Lights out)

(Lights switch back on to (A) kitchen area. FATHER has backed into MOTHER causing her to ruin the cake. Mother is standing, about to cry, as she holds up the tray that once held the birthday cake that is now smushed all over her dress. FATHER stands frozen, not knowing what to do)

MOTHER

Now look at what you've done! Darn it, how can we have a party without a cake? What has gotten into you today?

FATHER

(picks up a napkin to wipe the cake off MOTHER's dress)

Should I… go buy another one?

MOTHER

(bats FATHER away with her hands)

It's too late now… just… I'll figure something out. We don't have the time or money to buy another cake. It's almost six… that's when Dr. Ha said he was coming, right? It all ends today.

FATHER

I know.

MOTHER

Do you? Do you know that it wasn't easy for

me, being stuck in this role for twenty years? I'm old now! I want to see the world! You know what I mean?

FATHER

I think so.

MOTHER

I hope so! You make sure that we get what we deserve from that Dr. Ha today. It's our last chance, you hear me?

FATHER

Mhmm… I know what you're saying… I wonder what's going to happen to our boy after all this…

MOTHER

It's not our problem! He's a grown man! Whatever happens, whether it's working with Dr. Ha, or landing in a ditch somewhere, it just isn't our business anymore.

FATHER

I know, but still…

(Lights out. Lights switch back on in (B) ART's room. STELLA is nuzzling ART, and the couple attempts to finally kiss, but then the doorbell rings)

STELLA

(stands up and straightens her skirt)

Well... I guess that's it.

ART

Yep… that's it… for now.

STELLA

I should probably go home.

ART

No, please. I want you here, I need you here.

STELLA

Alright…

(looks at ART)

I've been meaning to tell you something…

ART

Yeah?

STELLA

Just promise me you won't be too surprised, yeah?

ART

What's up? Wait, this is serious, isn't it?

(holds STELLA's shoulders and looks into her eyes)

What'd I do, have I not kept a promise?
What's going on?

STELLA

Well… um… well… so, I am…

ART

Well, well. I haven't seen you so serious in… well, ever. First Pops, now you? Something is definitely up today.

STELLA

Look… the truth is… I hope you know…

(Doorbell rings twice this time)

STELLA

Even if we're apart… don't forget that I love you! I'll love you forever!

ART

Oh, sweetie…

STELLA

Remember how I feel about you, yeah?
No matter what happens.

ART

Listen. Nothing – no ocean, no college – can get between us. I'll be back before you know it. And... one day... if... when we get married... we'll always be together. So....

(Before he can finish, STELLA leaps into his arms. Lights out)

(Lights switch on in (A) kitchen and den area. Dr. Ha enters, examining the house as he walks in. MOTHER rushes to him, creating a scene with her overtly warm welcome)

MOTHER

O, Dr. Ha! Come in, come in, make yourself at home!

FATHER

Thank you for making it out here, to our humble abode.

DR. HA

Enough with the greetings, we must hurry! It's an emergency!

FATHER

(surprised)

An emergency?

MOTHER

(inquisitively)

What is going on Dr. Ha?

DR. HA

No time to explain. Quickly, bring the boy, we must leave at once.

MOTHER

Goodness, well, we all could use a couple minutes to sit down and catch our breath! While we have you here, Doctor, we have other matters we'd like to discuss with you.

DR. HA

Did you not hear me when I said it was an emergency? Now, if you may, please! The boy!

FATHER

(frantic)

The boy! Y-y-yes… ART! Can you come on out here?

(Lights switch on in (B) ART's room, while lights in (A) kitchen area stay on. ART is rubbing STELLA's shoulders as she holds back tears. ART carefully leads her out to the (A) kitchen area. Lights in (B) ART's room switch off)

(As ART and STELLA enter, DR. HA scrutinizes STELLA. She looks down at her feet to avoid eye contact with DR. HA)

ART

You were looking for me?

FATHER

Come say hello to Dr. Ha.

ART

(shakes his hand courteously)

Thank you for everything you've done for me. You've been very generous.

DR. HA

(walks around ART, checking him out from every angle)

You've grown up to be a fine young man.

ART

Thank you, sir, twenty today.

FATHER

Yes sir—off to college in America tomorrow!

DR. HA

Oh, I'm well aware.

(hesitates)

Before that though…

MOTHER

Sir, as you've seen, we've done our best all these years…

DR. HA

(interrupts her)

Yes, you've made your point abundantly clear. Now let me get mine across, will you?

(MOTHER moves away, standing behind FATHER)

DR. HA

I apologize for being abrupt, but we must leave at once. I'll explain more on the road.

ART

(surprised)

Leave?
Now?

STELLA

(shrieks)

Already?

(DR. HA looks at STELLA. ART looks at FATHER, seeking an explanation. FATHER hesitates for a second, then clears his throat)

FATHER

Dr. Ha… we were expecting him to leave tomorrow. His plane is booked, and I was planning on giving him a ride to the airport first thing in the morning. What harm could another night do, so we can have a proper goodbye?

DR. HA

A significant amount of harm. Mr. Oh's health has taken a turn for the worse.

FATHER

(eyes widen)

Oh, in that case, yes, yes, of course.

DR. HA

(turns towards ART)

Look, it is not my intention to alarm you. Mr. Oh is somebody that you absolutely must meet. After all, he is the one who has supported your education and upbringing till this day.

And now, he doesn't have much time. We just found out that he has stage IV pancreatic cancer... Another thing he shares with Steve Jobs, I guess! Anyway... his days are numbered. And he wants to spend at least one of those precious days with you before you leave for the States.

FATHER

(gets ART's jacket)

Oh yes, yes. What are we doing here then, let's get a move on! Artie boy. Son, without this man you wouldn't be...

(trails off without finishing and shakes it off)

Don't worry about your things, I'll send them to wherever you are.

ART

(furrows his brow)

Okay, Pops. Well, at least let me get my backpack.

(ART heads back to his room but stops when he notices STELLA standing still)

STELLA

I'll be right here, babe.

(ART turns and rushes to his room. Tension builds as the remaining four stand in silence. Finally, STELLA speaks to DR. HA)

STELLA

He was supposed to leave tomorrow.

MOTHER

That's fine, but we have some unfinished business, do we not? The last few payments... they haven't come through.

FATHER

(hushing her)

Hold on, we can discuss that later.

MOTHER

Absolutely not. This is an urgent matter for us. We have bills to pay!

DR. HA

You'll get a call soon.

FATHER

Yes, yes, of course.

(Father looks away, his hands folded in front of him. MOTHER glares at him, elbowing him to speak up, but Father ignores her request)

MOTHER

Seriously? You're going to be the death of me!
Pull the trigger, why don't you?
Do you think I gave up my life to raise some random kid from the kindness of my heart?
What do you take me for, a fool?

FATHER

Enough, I'm warning you!

(As FATHER looks up at MOTHER, he notices ART standing behind her, holding his backpack)

ART

Ma… what's that now?

MOTHER

(turns around and clears her throat)

Look, it's about time somebody told you the truth.

FATHER

(raises his voice)

I said, now is not the time!

DR. HA

(faces ART)

We really must go. What needs to be done has been done, and what needs to be said has been… I'll fill you in on the road.

(turns to Mother and Father)

Farewell for now then! Till our paths cross again. If… they cross again.

(ART takes a step forward, then frowns and looks back at STELLA)

ART

I'll call as soon as I can.

(ART and DR. HA exit)

MOTHER

(looking at the door, in a panic)

What are we going to do now? What a scam!

FATHER

(shouting)

For the love of God, shut up!
For the boy's sake, just shut the hell up!

(FATHER yells and throws his book to the ground. MOTHER, surprised at the unexpected outburst from her husband, shrinks back. STELLA breaks down in tears, collapsing onto the chair behind her)

LIGHTS OUT

SCENE 2

(The night lights of Seoul shimmer like stars, yet they are below the view from the high-rise penthouse. Above the skyscrapers, a white semicircle stage lights up in the center. MR. OH stands in the middle of the penthouse, holding a cane. DR. HA enters, followed by Art)

DR. HA

Apologies sir, it is late.

MR. OH

It's never too late to welcome you, my partner.

DR. HA

I've brought the boy.

MR. OH

Yes, of course. Welcome, young man.

It's been a while.

DR. HA

Well then, sir, I shall say goodnight.

MR. OH

It is quite late, indeed, go and get some rest

(takes a better look at DR. HA as he bids farewell)

My, you certainly could use some. Even the great scientist can't escape the hands of time, eh?

(chuckles)

We all know they haven't been kind to me either. I guess Time is the ultimate victor in this saga.

DR. HA

Yes indeed. I am sure the future we've worked for will happen. Worry not—goodnight and farewell.

MR. OH

Thank you, I appreciate it.

(DR. HA exits)

MR. OH :
(stares at ART)

Well, young man, don't just stand there! Come closer.

(ART steps closer into the circle. When he takes his eyes away from the view of the city and looks at MR. OH, he is shocked. The man standing before him is a mirror image of himself)

ART

How… h-how could this be?

MR. OH

I'd be just as surprised if I were you. I know all there is to know, and yet I can't help being a little… nervous right now. Unfortunately, we don't have much time to ease into things.

ART
(nervous)

Who… are you?

MR. OH

You, in a way. We share the same DNA.

ART

The same?

MR. OH

Identical.

(The lights fade out, tightening onto the two faces on stage. It creates the illusion that nothing except for two floating faces exists)

ART

How could it be? How could we be so… alike? Your face, your eyes, your voice! Even your hands. It can't be, it's impossible! Am I hallucinating? Is this all a dream? Another nightmare?

MR. OH

This is certainly a reality. You and I…

ART

We share the same DNA? Does that make us… family?

MR. OH

Not by my definition.

ART

Does that make you… my father?

MR. OH

No.

ART

(holding back tears, talking to himself)

Does that make me… what does that make me?

MR. OH

I heard you want to be a geneticist and work in Biotech one day. It's a great idea. You don't need a degree to understand what's happening here.

ART

How could it be…? What does that make me… to you?

(ART breaks down sobbing. MR. OH is silent)

ART

(crying in anger)

Tell me… the truth!

MR. OH

It's been twenty years already. Dr. Ha had successfully cloned animals and announced it to the world. The world didn't take the news well and desperately opposed him. Some hid down in Jeju Island, your hometown, and continued their research. They needed a sponsor, and I was willing to fund them.

You see, my legacy is my work, but it has left me with no family, no offspring. I wanted to leave my mark in time, a memory of the future. After many trials and errors, we were successful. Someone gave the name 'ART' to your life.

ART

That's all I am? A work of art? Just another clone, like Dolly the lamb? What is my purpose? To be a bag of spare parts?

MR. OH

(shakes his head vigorously)

No, no, no, not at all. That was never my intention.

ART

The clones... something always went wrong with them. What is wrong with me? What will go wrong with me?

MR. OH

If that were the case, wouldn't you know by now? The shock seems to have clouded your reasoning.

ART

So, you're saying... I wasn't created to be harvested.

MR. OH

No, certainly I do not consider you an extension of me. We may have the same set of DNA, but you have cultivated your mind, your soul! You are a unique being!

(lights fade back into the penthouse)

ART

Yet… I haven't been created naturally. I wasn't born out of love!

MR. OH

Does it matter how we got here?
What matters is that we are here.

ART

So, you're saying… I am the same as any other being out there.

MR. OH

Absolutely! No different from any other man walking down the street. Look at Mt. Olympus! Some Greek gods were born from Zeus' thigh or his forehead. In a way, you're like… Adam, the first of his kind.

ART

But…

MR. OH

Mankind has yet to tap into the fountain of wisdom. Now it will happen in the not-too-distant, inevitable future...

ART

(interrupts)

Why hasn't anyone spoken about this before? How can it be...?

MR. OH

We couldn't take the risk. If anybody had found out, both our lives would be in jeopardy, I'm sure you can understand.

ART

(talking to himself)

What right... do you think you have...

MR. OH

(continues as if he hadn't heard ART)

It wasn't a smooth ride, rather, a fearful one. Even we couldn't believe what we had pulled off—this was greater than any revolution mankind had been through!

Our work was constantly being tracked, and the critics were watching incessantly. Had we been found? We wouldn't be standing here.

I had to keep you safe, and the only way was to hide you in plain sight. Those who opposed our work, in the name of tradition, would never guess to look for you there. And believe me, they're still out there, searching.

ART

Who is? Where?

MR. OH

My fear may be speaking here, but these people are extremely hostile. Yet despite that, I had to meet you. I don't have much time left, but I need to spend it telling you the truth. Believe me.

ART

So, all the financial support these years, it was you, not Dr. Ha.

MR. OH

Dr. Ha and I have worked together for a long time. It was simply a safer set of hands.

ART

(slowly nodding, finally acquiescing)

My parents and I have always been grateful.

MR. OH

Listen carefully, young man. The human body, no matter what it's made of or how it's created, is merely a conduit for what matters – the human soul. Sure, doctors of all fields could interject in the birthing process, but the lighting of the soul is where the ultimate mystery awaits. Science cannot touch that.

(The intercom beeps, and the voice of Mr. Oh's secretary comes through)

SECRETARY
(voice only)

Sir, Mr. Bezos is on the line.

MR. OH

What does Jeff want at this late hour?

SECRETARY

He says it's urgent, sir.

MR. OH

Whatever it is, it can wait.

SECRETARY

Yes, sir.

(MR. OH turns around and walks towards his desk, opens a drawer and takes out a small, gift-wrapped box)

MR. OH

Happy birthday. Here, take it.

(ART carefully unwraps it to find an antique compass, shaped as a half-dome, with a laurel wreath etched around it)

ART

This seems… like an heirloom.

MR. OH

It has always belonged in my family. You will be embarking on your life's journey from this moment forward, and from what I can see, you will need some guidance.

ART

I'll treasure it.

MR. OH

We never board the ship of life knowing the destination. Yet if this can provide comfort during the lonely voyage, it will have served its purpose.

ART

(breaths deeply, more at ease)

So... I hear you are unwell.

MR. OH

This body might be wasting away, but I am a warrior. Even if Troy falls tomorrow, I shall fight till the end.

ART

However, everything rises and falls, sir.

MR. OH

We can only do our best with what little time we are given. I must admit, there was a time when I wished for you to continue my work, to carry on with my role. The idea of you, another me of the next generation, continuing my legacy! It was a marvelous thought. A thought that lit fire to the experiment.

ART

Do I have a choice?

MR. OH

Unfortunately, you do, regardless of my wishes.

ART

Thank you for respecting that.

MR. OH

My kingdom of Troy may be a matter of life and death for me, but it could mean nothing to you. It took me a long time and a wretched disease to realize that. You are your own being, regardless of your gene pool. A more astonishing fact is that just because we share the same DNA, doesn't mean we're the same human being. Art, you are unique, regardless of your DNA.

(The intercom beeps again)

SECRETARY

Sir, sir! There are some people out here, and…

(Before she can finish, the line is cut and the power shuts off, as if someone pulled the plug)

LIGHTS OUT

SCENE 3

(The clock strikes midnight as the stage lights up dimly. All is grey except for the semicircle stage in the middle, which is now pitch black. What was white is now black, and what used to be sky-high is now deep underground. It is unknown whether this space is a basement, a cave, or a prison cell)

(Gradually, the opposing party appears through the dark, lighting up candles one by one, filling up the outline of the semicircle. In the dark, each candle lights up an angry face, creating a grotesque picture. Amidst the faces, a grey light reveals ART AND MR. OH, waking up to find themselves in changed surroundings)

ART

(still groggy)

Where am I… What… Who are you?

MR. OH

What is this? What the hell is going on?

(The opposing party members place their candles on the ground, revealing themselves. They all don black cloaks and resemble each other in appearance. LORD stands in the center, with LEFT HAND and RIGHT HAND guarding him on each side)

RIGHT HAND

(in an authoritative tone)

Silence! You are here to judge!

LEFT HAND

Indeed! You are here to implement justice.

ART

Judge? Justice? To whom? For what?

RIGHT HAND

Silence! Who else can it be but you two!

MR. OH

Such unwelcome words from such unwelcome guests.

ART

Yeah! Who are you to have that right?

RIGHT HAND

We are those who wish to save humanity.

LEFT HAND

We are the ones who want to protect this Earth from danger.

ART

Am I, as an individual, the enemy of mankind? What have I done to harm you? To harm humanity?

MR. OH

Tell me what the grandiose crime you're accusing us of. I'm listening.

RIGHT HAND

Imitating God is dangerous! It is a crime to pretend to be God.

LEFT HAND

It is a line not to be crossed, a realm not to be entered. An act that humans should never attempt!

ART

No, no, I've done nothing of the sort. I was thrown into the world, to exist this way. I was just thrown into.

MR. OH

It's true. He's not to blame.

RIGHT HAND

Silence! He is the product of your sins, the axis of your wrongdoing, the damning evidence!

MR. OH

Wait, wait. Who gave you guys the authority to wield violence?

LEFT HAND

We are the voice of the majority, the messenger of the sacred! The ultimate authority against the blasphemous! Empowered by the state, by public opinion, by the fear of all.

ART

What? What pretext did you say? Authorized by who?

RIGHT HAND

In the name of God!

LEFT HAND & REST OF OPPOSING PARTY

(in unison)

Amen!

ART

Ah, come to think of it, it is you guys who are

attempting to imitate God! Talking about blasphemy and pretending to be God?

(Art smirks, LORD takes a step forward into the center)

LORD

(scolding voice)

Such insolence! Such disrespect from... a freak! There was no rib, no sperm, no act of love involved in your birth. God did not grant his permission in the creation of your life! Your existence alone is sacrilegious!

(MR. OH stands up and takes a step forward, standing face-to-face with LORD)

MR. OH

With all due respect, to give you my opinion on what you just said, our Savior Jesus was born through the power of the Holy Spirit.... He also didn't need a man's sperm. Isn't that so?

RIGHT HAND

Sacrilege!

LEFT HAND

You shall pay for taking the Lord's name in vain, Sinner!

LORD

(shouting)

Who dares to toy with the sacred right of birth? You shall pay for your sins, mocking the ultimate command by intercepting the holy creation of life! By insulting the dignity of mankind! By murdering the many lives created under your microscope! It is against every law of nature, the worst of crimes!

(LORD growls like a wild beast, yet MR. OH does not even flinch)

MR. OH

We have done nothing of the sort. We have committed no crime. All we have done is further build upon the work that nature had already begun. Our work is an extension of the science behind identical twins, or horticultural grafting. Does it come with risk? Or course. The reckless nature of mankind creates that risk.

What we have done is everything but against the laws of nature. The furthest thing possible from blasphemy.

(As he pauses, MR.OH's final words echo throughout the dark space)

RIGHT HAND

Silence! Still has a lot of say!

LEFT HAND

Insolence! Still doesn't know what his sin is!

LORD

Are you so blind to see the extent of your sins?

MR. OH

I am fully aware of my doings and of its implications. I was passionate in my pursuit, acutely conscious, and chose willingly.

LORD

He speaks with the tongue of the devil! Pursuing human progress? No, you rushed to our demise. You have brought us closer to the future indeed, nearer our extinction! The reckless nature of mankind? Speak for yourself!

MR. OH

Did God ever stop creating? You cannot prevent the future from happening. You cannot hold back the hands of time.

LORD

Remember this! All crooked deviation comes at a cost.

MR. OH

I couldn't agree more. And still, I ask, who are you to determine what is right or wrong? Don't we all get to make our own choices at endless turning points?

LORD

Look! Isn't this obvious, your choice has brought that young man to the brink of his death! So, tell me, is that right or wrong?

MR. OH

Look again! Isn't it you who are disclaiming responsibility despite meddling in the flow of civilization? What will be the cause of this so-called death? Speak for yourself! You are the ones imposing yourselves into another man's nature, artificially changing the destiny of one's predestined fate. Yet you toss the blame to others!

RIGHT HAND

Doesn't bend even a little bit.

LEFT HAND

Doesn't acknowledge his sins even a little bit.

ART

What do you mean, sins? I never asked to come to this world. All I can remember is being delivered here. Unexpectedly... without knowing why exactly. I was placed on this earth just like the rest of you. I heard that the method of my conception was different. But could you fault me for that? Should I now pay with my life for the way life was given to me?

RIGHT HAND

Still rude!

LEFT HAND

Still resistant!

LORD

As you have pointed out, your roots of origin are the root of the problem. You didn't come into existance legitimately. Because of you, the order of nature has been disturbed, and because of you, society will be in peril. For you have brought chaos to the sacred code of human life!

ART

Because of me?
You speak as if I had a say in it!

LORD

Right! Your existence alone suggests that one can infinitely copy and paste life. That one can build an entire army from one man. That man is limitless! When that hope is placed in the hands of the ill-willed, our world as we know it falls in jeopardy. We are trying now to prevent that danger beforehand. You understand? It's very dangerous for fools to control life as they wish, all on their own.

RIGHT HAND

Thus, human cloning is as dangerous as nuclear weapons!

LEFT HAND

Thus, cloning is wrong—it is murder!

LORD

Thus, we forbid it.

ART

Wait, wait! The way you all speak... who's the clone now, eh? Repeating the same thing to that degree.

RIGHT HAND

How dare you insult us?

LEFT HAND

How dare you insult justice?

MR. OH

Hold it with the petty insults and long-winded excuses—those are the weapons of the weak. The point is... this young man here is innocent. I may not have been the one to create him in the lab, but I made it my responsibility when I provided my genes.

LORD

(laughing)

Take responsibility? Ha!
The nerve! What impudence!

MR. OH

Think about it! Have you ever been successful in bending, or preventing the will of man from doing what they wanted to do? Look back through the pages of history! Too much blood has been spilt already.

LORD

History repeats itself. Just look at how we stand here, face to face, once again.

MR. OH

Alas, we meet again. Aren't you tired of this battle, spanning decades, no, centuries? When will you let it go, my medieval foe?

LORD

Alas.

(LORD laughs loudly, shaking his entire body. RIGHT HAND pulls out a shiny neon-colored gun from his cloak. LORD holds up his hand, motioning him to stop)

LORD

Leave it.
No need to be rash and hurried!
We still have time.

RIGHT HAND

We have no more time to waste!

LEFT HAND

We cannot let them escape!

RIGHT HAND

It's dangerous!

LEFT HAND

They are dangerous!

RIGHT HAND & LEFT HAND
(in unison)

Human beings are not to be trusted!

LORD
(sternly)

Silence! Don't define everything so recklessly! Man is undefinable. Humans are vague beings. The earth and heavens, the good and the evil. Maybe God even exists in that young man. For God is the creator and what he does is... creation.

RIGHT HAND & LEFT HAND
(in unison)

God is the creator of all.

(LORD walks to the back of the stage and lifts his arms towards heaven, in worship. RIGHT HAND and LEFT HAND do the same, as do the rest. As the followers stand still in their prolonged prayer, ART and MR. OH huddle together)

ART
(whispers to MR. OH)

I fear for what is about to happen.

MR. OH

Art, stand back and let me take it from here.

ART

I'm scared, but I want to stand up, too!

MR. OH

This is my responsibility. It is my burden to bear... mine alone to carry.

ART

I didn't have a say in my creation, but I'd readily die to have the choice in my demise.

MR. OH

Now is not the time to choose!

ART

We can always choose!

MR. OH

Please, I beg of you. For my sake, please wait, one last time.

(ART hesitates, pausing for a moment to think)

Take it as my dying word, my final will to you. I shall point the way out when the time comes. Follow my direction, one last time.

ART

...fine.

MR. OH

Remember. We all have our dreams to follow.

(LORD and CREW break out of their worshipping, roaring like wild beasts)

LORD

Mark my words, I shall show no mercy!
I do not want to repeat the same mistake!
Copernicus be damned!

RIGHT HAND

The radicals shall burn at the stake!

LEFT HAND

The death sentence to those who covet the realm of God!

LORD

Silence! I too am merely the executioner. Nothing is up to us – we simply carry the message and follow His will. The order has already been written; the final decision has been made.

(directing RIGHT HAND and LEFT HAND)

It is time. Now take them away.

(RIGHT HAND and LEFT HAND pull out their guns and point them at the backs of ART and MR.OH, motioning them to walk out. MR. OH pretends to comply but then charges at RIGHT HAND. He manages to wrangle RIGHT HAND's gun out of its grasp and points it towards LORD's head. Everybody backs away. MR. OH signals to ART)

MR. OH

Art, it is time! The exit is on that side!

ART

Ah, Mr. Oh!

MR. OH

Run towards the light, my son!

(ART takes a deep breath, then runs off the stage. LORD, RIGHT HAND, and LEFT HAND remain still, as MR.OH points the gun at LORD's head. He takes a step forward. RIGHT HAND and LEFT HAND stand still, whimpering)

RIGHT HAND
(crys out)

We were only trying to keep our society safe and sound!

LEFT HAND
(crys out)

We were only following orders from our superiors!

(RIGHT HAND and LEFT HAND tremble in fear as MR. OH takes another step closer. Suddenly MR.OH stops and points the gun at himself)

MR. OH

I shall pay the price for my choices. However, the future is already on my side.

(He pulls the trigger, falling to the ground. As he hits the floor, a loud thud echoes through the stage. As ART runs past, the candles flicker furiously. One candle remains lit next to MR. OH's body)

(lengthy pause)

(Two gunshots sound in the distance. There is no telling who's been hit)

(lengthy pause)

(The mournful tune of Max Richter's 'Sarajevo' plays in the background. The grey light over MR. OH's dead body fades to black)

LIGHTS OUT

SCENE 4

(An unknown place, at an unknown hour of the night)

(The entire stage is dark. Throughout this scene, only faces float around in the dark, giving the audience a glimpse into a fabricated world)

(DR. HA enters, his face floats over to the center of the stage, and a quick knocking sound is heard. LORD's face appears. He is calm, closing his eyes. At the sound of the knock, he opens his eyes and speaks in a low, baritone voice)

LORD

Come in, I've been waiting for you.

DR. HA

Is everything resolved?

LORD

It appears so. Here, take this.
Your money is on the table.

(DR. HA searches for his promised fee. Once he finds it, he turns to the other side and rummages through his bag. The sound of a thick binder being dropped onto the table is heard. LORD looks down to check the files. DR. HA takes a step back and bows politely)

DR. HA

May you have infinite glory.

LORD

You have completed the great experiment of nineteen years. You know, that Frankenstein character disappeared the day he was born. As if he never existed. Now that we know human beings can be cloned, and our mission is fully accomplished. Let's keep it just between us and close the door on the matter.

DR. HA

Of course, just between us.

LORD

Indeed, this stays between us.

(pauses in thought for a moment)

I shall take these confidential files and keep them in a safe place.

DR. HA;

That sounds right!

(bows politely)

Then I'll say my goodbyes here.

LORD

Exactly. That will be all, Doc!

(DR. HA bows once again and starts to walk out. He stops, as if remembering something, and turns back to LORD)

DR. HA

By the way, did you want to meet… the others?

(LORD contemplates for a moment, then nods)

LORD

Ah… yes. Bring them.

DR. HA

Alright. I shall bring them in soon.

(DR. HA exits. LORD waits until he leaves, then clicks his tongue with a frustrated sigh)

LORD

Hmm, hmmm, that bastard is the wild card, isn't he? What am I going to do about him? Too difficult to read, too smart for his good! A loose cannon, that one. Should I go ahead and cut the rope? Or wait a little longer, and see? Decisions, decisions!

(The same quick knocking sound from earlier is heard again. DR. HA re-enters the stage, followed by a nervous FATHER and an eager MOTHER. STELLA drags her heels behind them, blowing bubbles with her chewing gum)

LORD

Come in, come in. You've had a long journey.

MOTHER
(in a cheerful voice)

By long journey, if you mean it took us two decades to get here, you're right, it's been a long trip! Oh, the stress that came with it! And the costs! Don't worry, I've been keeping all the receipts, itemized. There were some… extra expenses that occurred outside of the original deal. I'm sure you understand. We've done nothing but stay true to the cause for twenty long years.

(FATHER bites his lip, his eyes scanning the room. STELLA pops a bubble loudly but makes no eye contact with anyone. FATHER hesitates, then clears his throat)

FATHER

Oh, yes, we have a contract. A deal is a deal, and we did our job. No, I mean, we tried our best to remain faithful to your mission. Although...

LORD

You have questions to be answered?

FATHER

Y-y-yes... sir... Mmhmmm, mhmm.

LORD

Well then, do not hesitate. Go on! Speak up!

FATHER

What... what I don't... that, I'm sorry, Hmm... Ahem, what I cannot fully comprehend... is that... how... how could the child, no, the clone I mean, potentially harm us? Harm our future?

(FATHER pauses, looks around nervously to read the room)

I apologize. W-w-what I meant, what I mean

is... Ahem... I mean... yes... I've raised the boy, I mean, I played the role of his father his whole life... and from what I could gather... he was the same. The same as any other child. The same as us.

LORD

And your point is?

FATHER

Forgive me for my ignorance, but I don't understand why it was such a crime against God's will to start with. Besides, the boy was kind-hearted, a good kid... and he had to be...we had to... all for what?

STELLA
(steps forward)

True. Art was good, no, wonderful! He never doubted us for a moment.

MOTHER

Oh, my gosh! Utter nonsense! He was a product of sin, crafted by the Nazis, there is no good in that! We cannot invite the Nazi demons to run amuck. I'd rather see our world blasted to bits with a nuclear weapon before that happens!

(DR. HA breaks his silence, taking a step forward and shaking his head. He raises an eyebrow, with an annoyed expression as he speaks)

DR. HA

If… I may. Let's set the record straight… shall we? There is no need to go… into details, but we should at least steer in the right… direction. First and foremost, I am not the… devil. I am no Nazi either, let's keep that clear. I am a man of science, and yes, we are responsible for starting this… headache.

But it's not right to fault us… to blame us. We are men of science, and we work, no, we strive for mankind. We simply mean to unveil the hidden truths of nature, to understand the meaning behind each step. Science is not to blame, but human nature is! In the wrong hands, this simple experiment could become power. It could become war. It could become a disaster. All we are doing is cleaning up after our work, to prevent such outcomes in advance.

LORD

That's right. Only God is deserving of such power. It is the job of us, the faithful, to come together to preserve and protect His right.

STELLA

Then why bother dragging it out so long?
Could've ended everything at birth. I mean,
I'm not complaining about the twenty-year-
long gig, but still, why?

MOTHER

It was a grand, twenty-year act on stage. One deserving of a standing ovation, a worthy reward.

FATHER

It wasn't just an act. It was honest work for a greater purpose.

STELLA

Honest?
We've been living a lie this whole time,
and you call that honest work?

MOTHER

Whatever you call it, it was a job well done.
We got paid and we still have some checks to come.

(LORD clears his throat to silence the three, stepping into the middle)

LORD

Indeed, a job well done. Your hard work these past years is greatly appreciated. Without your faith and devotion, this mission to save humanity would not have been successful. We could not do it without you. It wouldn't have been possible with just Dr. Ha.

MOTHER

Of course, of course!

(looking sideways towards DR. HA)

He was cold-hearted. We all knew the doctor couldn't have pulled it off on his own.

DR. HA

(offended)

I can't help but say something as you're still taking stabs in the dark. Open your eyes and listen, you nitwits! I haven't done anything on my own, and none of this is for me! I too, am a mere servant, a messenger of a greater purpose, don't you see? As we all are,

(looking at LORD)

wouldn't you agree?

(LORD clears his throat again, silencing DR. HA)

LORD

Well, well. Now it is time to close this door shut. Let's just say we are all just servants, serving His purpose, for humanity. There is only one all-knowing being, and it is not our place to know more.

(At LORD'S words, FATHER and MOTHER bow their heads politely, acquiescing. DR. HA pauses as if he is about to say something. He changes his mind, holds back and looks down. STELLA snorts and spits her gum out. She steps forward with a look of determination)

STELLA

So then, what are you going to do about this one? The one growing inside me?

FATHER
(surprised)

In you?

MOTHER
(rolling her eyes)

The sass on this one! You just had to get yourself knocked up? You had to go off-script?

DR. HA

That... was not part of the... project.

LORD

Well, that's surprising. Quite unexpected. Indeed, there's always a surprise twist in human affairs and there's always a setback in plans.

STELLA

It's the result of my best efforts!

MOTHER

(snorts)

Then it's simple, isn't it?
Erase it!

STELLA

But this child was created from nature! It is His will!

MOTHER

Are you certain, by the way?

STELLA

Hello! The things you say!
I'm a faithful person, too.

MOTHER

Seemed to me that His directions were clear, and it didn't include a sequel! We cannot fight amongst ourselves... we who believe.

STELLA

For once, we can agree!

LORD

You know, abortion is not allowed. You are aware of that.

STELLA

What should I do then?

LORD

You need to raise it. As is my will. After all, life is a gift.

STELLA
(dumbfounded)

A gift? For Whom? Who will be in charge of it?

FATHER
(hopeful and eager)

Why don't we take it? We can raise it!
A new beginning, a second act!

MOTHER

Has this old man finally lost his mind?
You'll be the death of me!

STELLA

(with tender maternal eyes)

Pfft, don't worry, there will be none of that. I'm going to raise it. Because it's my baby. No matter what anybody says, I'm going to love it to bits. Because it is our baby! Art's and mine.

LORD

Up to you! My job is done, and I have run out of time here. The play you have been doing, a part of it is over. It is time to move on to the next job. Come on, let's all go. The next stage is waiting. There is too much to do in this world, we must hurry!

(LORD exits the stage, followed by DR. HA, FATHER, and MOTHER. STELLA starts to walk out, then stops)

(Max Richter's 'On the Nature of Daylight' starts to play in the background. The pin-light that was only showing Stella's face, widens, now shining on her face and her torso. Her arms cradle her stomach, which now has a single flower decoration in the center of her belly)

STELLA

Everything's going to be alright, baby. It's gonna be alright.I know. You know. The heavens know that we loved each other. That what we had was real. That he was real.

(switching her tone to one of contempt)

A clone? A freak? Can't be my Art.
In a world full of pseudo-humans, parrot humans, copycat humans—a world full of chaos, my Art was nothing but truthful. Nobody was more real than…

(softening again)

him, my darling. Oh, I'll be fine, I'll be alright. I'm gonna stay strong. To grow you, baby, to birth you baby, to take care of you till the end, my baby. I'll teach you what it is to be human, to live your truth.We may live like clouds, simply floating above the Earth, without creating a wrinkle in mankind's time. But you, my baby, you'll be great. You'll have me by your side. Till the end.

O, Art, my love.
My darling little… work of Art.

(STELLA cradles her stomach with maternal lovingness, the shadowy figure of ART lights up in the back of the stage as if a figment of her imagination. He carries his backpack and holds a candle. He stares at STELLA and glides off the stage)

(The lights fade out until all that can be seen is the candle that ART was holding. It flickers in the wind as the music ends)

LIGHTS OUT & CURTAIN

I am part of all that I have met.

—Alfred Lord Tennyson

VAGABONDS

Death to Anti-Romance

THE PLAYERS

ZERO
Young man in his twenties

OLD MAN
Ninety-year-old man, frail and haggard, of unknown origin

BOY
Nine-year-old boy

GENERAL URSINE
General of an ancient army that worships the Bear
(The General is followed by his army, which could be either real or computer graphics projected on the stage)

GENERAL TIGRIS
General of an ancient army that worships the Tiger
(The General is followed by his army, which could be either real or computer graphics projected on the stage)

FEMALE
Young woman in her twenties works for City Hall as a secretary

MAYOR-BOT
Robot that rules the city

POLICE-BOT & DOCTOR-BOT

SHADOW
Mysterious observer appears on stage but doesn't speak

(He could be ZERO's ego, or OLD MAN in a different body, or one's subconscious in a dream)

SCENE 1

(The scene begins at a bus stop by the Han River. There is a bus stop sign, and a puddle of rain, in front of an old tree)

(OLD MAN squats next to the sign, dozing off. The old man looks as though he could collapse with the slightest breeze)

(ZERO enters, wearing a white T-shirt and jeans, and gripping the strap of his guitar bag. He looks towards the sun, squinting, looks down with a scowl and shakes his head. Pulls his guitar out and begins to sing a song of angst and defiance)

ZERO'S SONG

No, no, no, can't stand it anymore
Might as well stick your head to the floor
Under a sky full of nothing but filth
No room to grow, just doomed to wilt
Ah-ah-ah death to romance, death to love

No matter where you look, darkness above
We've painted the town gold
Buildings scraping the sky
But we've lost our light, forgotten how to fly.

(ZERO's guitar solo comes to an end. OLD MAN wakes and rubs his eyes, looks at ZERO and clicks his tongue in annoyance)

OLD MAN

Tsk, tsk. Can't find a quiet spot somewhere else?

ZERO

Well, I can't find a reason to live anymore!

OLD MAN

Young people and their complaints.

ZERO

Look around old man. Is this a place worth living for?

OLD MAN

What's wrong with it? I don't find anything wrong except me!

ZERO

You look up, and all you see are skyscrapers. You look down and see filth, trash, and mud at your feet. You take a deep breath, but with all the pollution you can hardly inhale. Everywhere you look, it's just grey, grey, grey! What's a guy like me supposed to look forward to?

OLD MAN

Excuses, excuses.

(OLD MAN shifts his weight and holds on to the tree, groaning as he pulls himself up. He strokes the rough bark of the tree, and starts to sing in a deep croaky voice)

OLD MAN'S SONG I

Where else would we be, where else but here
We reach for the sky but are no place near
You've laid down your roots, all these years
Listened to our noise, our screams and tears
The tongue of man is the deadliest weapon
Inhaling every gift Mother Earth has given
Exhaling nothing but sin after sin
We deserve punishment, we deserve no wins.

OLD MAN
(talking to the tree)

Wouldn't you agree, my resilient tree?

(OLD MAN puts his bare foot in the puddle, moves it back and forth making ripples and smiles. He sings)

OLD MAN'S SONG II

Nothing but sky above
Nothing but earth below
Here stands a man in between
Stuck with nowhere to go
Invited by no one, he arrived on his own
Can't remember what brought him here
Now he's lost... lost and all alone.

OLD MAN
(talks to the puddle)

Wouldn't you agree, my black-mirrored friend?

(OLD MAN looks at ZERO, scrutinizes him, asks a question)

OLD MAN

So, what do they call you young man?

ZERO

Zero.

OLD MAN
(rubbing his ear, trying to hear better)

Zeee...z....zeeeee... like you're asleep?

ZERO

No, not Z the letter. Zero is the number.

Meaning nothing... and everything.

OLD MAN
(rubbing his ear again)

Oh, Xerox! Like the copying machine!

ZERO

Never mind. If you can't hear that well, you probably won't remember that well either. Just call me... a vagabond.

OLD MAN
(hears correctly this time)

A vagabond? Ha! That adds up.

(OLD MAN walks around ZERO, his hands clasped behind his back, checking him out thoroughly. He pauses a moment to think. Suddenly, an idea comes to him)

OLD MAN

Your fate could use a little tweaking.
Hand me your hand!

ZERO
(dubious)

I don't believe in that superstitious stuff.

OLD MAN

Superstition is a belief as well! Hence, I don't believe in anything.

ZERO

So... we agree that nothing is nothing.

OLD MAN

The only thing we can agree on is that we know nothing. So enough with the talking, it's time to start seeing!

(OLD MAN turns his back to ZERO, then starts to pull out objects from his pockets. Out comes an old scroll of parchment, a calligraphy pen, a pair of scissors, a glue stick, and a bottle of liquor accompanied by a shot glass. He pours himself a glass and takes a quick sip. He then pours another, says a quick prayer and pours the drink out as an offering. He puts his hands together politely, and begins an incantation)

OLD MAN

Abracadabra, Alakazam, Hocus pocus, Sim Sala Ba... Oh, I forgot to add something of slime and filth.

(OLD MAN takes the shot glass, squats by the puddle, and scoops up the muddy water. He mixes it with liquor, takes a sip then offers the glass to ZERO, who has been staring in disbelief. Zero grimaces and shakes his head in refusal)

OLD MAN

I take it that's a hard no! Alright. Now put your hands together, palms facing up.

ZERO

(still dubious, does as he is told)

Whatever this pagan ritual is, I'm not buying it!

(OLD MAN ignores him, unrolls the scroll and starts writing with a calligraphy pen. Then takes scissors and cuts the scroll into four pieces. He glues two pieces of paper on ZERO's eyes and two on ZERO's palms. Takes muddy liquor from the glass and sprinkles it on each parchment, like a chef adding the final touches of seasoning to a dish)

OLD MAN

Now, look into your hands. What do you see?

ZERO

(eyes still covered with paper)

Zero. Nil. Nada. Nothing.

OLD MAN

Nothing at all?

ZERO

(tilts his head)

Nothing! At all!

OLD MAN

Tsk, tsk. You're so blind! So unreceptive! How can somebody, as young as you, have

such a rigid mind? It's not only that you can't see, you're blind to new ideas.
Come on! Open your eyes!

ZERO

(touching the pieces of paper stuck to his eyes)

Um... what are these? Have you blindsided me, old man?

OLD MAN

Ah! Now those!
Those are your golden tickets, your break-out-of-jail cards—it's a free ride, F-R-E-E!
So, dust off your cobwebbed brain, and think.
Where do you want to go? Because when you have a strong will, there will be a way.

ZERO

I already told you, I'm not buying any of it!

(rips the paper from his eyes and palms, throws them on the ground)

Look, as thrilling as it's made out to be... these adventures into space, or twilight zones, beyond whatever dull reality we're stuck in... I have a hard time believing any of it... to me, these illusions are nothing but child play. Grow up, old man!

OLD MAN

(mutters to himself)

Tsk, tsk. Oh, it was too much to expect! Without an understanding of how much he could handle! Proof that foolishness is bound to the young heart, not the young at heart.

OLD MAN

(faces ZERO)

Now, listen up young man. Use this ticket as if your life depends on it. Remember, it's free, F-R-E-E. That's the password and code. It's free, so use it as you please—it'll cost you nothing.

(quietly under his breath)

Or everything.

(back to his louder tone)

Remember that! Farewell.

(OLD MAN exits off stage. ZERO, unsure of what to do, stands dumbfounded. He looks down at the ground, picks up the pieces of paper he had thrown away. As he reaches for the pieces of paper, they float into the air and flutter like butterflies)

(The audience can't see it, but the paper is tied to fishing lines controlled by OLD MAN)

ZERO

(flailing about, trying to grab the paper)

Wh-wh-what? My tickets!

OLD MAN
(voice echoing from a distance)

Spells, hexes, chants, prayers… they're all just words!

(From a distance, ZERO looks like he's chasing butterflies. He spins in circles like a dog chasing its tail. He flaps and jumps like a chicken trying to fly. He keeps his eyes on the tickets as he follows them off stage. Soon after, a loud splash is heard, as he falls into the Han River)

ZERO

H-h-h-help!

(The stage is empty. ZERO's voice echoes from afar)

OLD MAN
(cheerfully)

It won't be a long journey! You should be back before sunset. I shall see you then! Oh, and I hope you know how to swim!
I forgot to ask.

(OLD MAN's echoes slowly fade out. All that can be heard are desperate splashes from the river)

LIGHTS OUT

SCENE 2

(Transported through time, the bus stop in front of Han River is now an ancient battlefield)

(ZERO enters, with his eyes closed. The steady beat of war drums can be heard in the distance, slowly growing louder. As the drums boom closer, ZERO opens his eyes. He jumps back, shell-shocked when he finds two armies surging around)

(Now he is standing between two armies: the Ursine Army, holding flags with the image of a bear, and the Tigris army, holding up flags with an image of a roaring Tiger. The soldiers are lined up in formation, behind their leaders, General Ursine and General Tigris, as if each army is a mirror of the other)

(Soldiers march to the drum of the beat. ZERO freaks out, as the Tigris Army begins to sing and dance their war song)

SONG OF TIGRIS

Listen to the roar of the mighty tiger
The Lord of the Mountain
The winning survivor
Ever so righteous, fast and astute
You'll never beat us—surrender, salute
We mark our land with our razor-sharp claw
Invaders beware, the fangs in our jaws
For this is our nation, and we're here to stay
Bow down to our roars, go ahead, make way!

(As the Tigris Army roars with passion, the beat picks up and the Ursine Army marches forward)

SONG OF URSINE

Stomp! Stomp! Stomp! Stomp!
The earth shakes in despair
There's no one grander
Than the almighty Ursine bear
You've never seen strength
Till you've felt Ursine muscle
We're brave and we're tough
The ultimate hustle
One swipe of a paw, and mountains collapse
A breath turns the ocean current
Quick as a snap
Step aside, kneel and bow to your new king
Stomp and join us on the Ursine awakening.

(As the Ursine Army's song comes to an end, the drums beat loudly and soldiers rally on both sides, marching in unison. Amidst the frenzy, ZERO finds himself in the middle of the Tigris Army. He joins them as one)

SONG OF THE BATTLE FIELD

(GENERALS)

Forward! Forward! March to victory

(SOLDIERS)

Stab and destroy, we're in for the kill

(GENERALS)

Wave your flag high, Swing your swords

(SOLDIERS)

Stab and destroy, we're in for the kill

(GENERALS)

Mount your horses as arrows fly

(SOLDIERS)

Stab and destroy, we're in for the kill

(GENERALS)

Onward! Onward! The bravest, the greatest

(SOLDIERS)

Stab and destroy, we're in for the kill.

(After the last line ends, both armies hold up their swords and scream war cries, ready to charge at each other. ZERO comes to his senses and jumps in between the two armies, ready to interfere)

ZERO

Stop! Stop! Stop! Cease fire!

(Both armies pause. The war drums stop. All stand still in silence)

ZERO

(pointing at the Ursine Army)

I know who they are. They're all… family.

GENERAL TIGRIS

What is this you speak of? Family?

ZERO

We're of the same bloodline. We're all related. We're of the same blood.
We all bleed.

GENERAL TIGRIS

Nonsense! We shall rid our sacred land of those barbarians! We must fight!
We must kill!

SOLDIERS OF TIGRIS ARMY

Stab and destroy! We're in for the kill!

ZERO

No, I refuse to fight a fellow brother!

GENERAL TIGRIS

(roaring at his army)

I will not tolerate this disobedience!
Bring forth the insubordinate!

(SHADOW enters quietly. He stands in the corner without a word, simply observing)

GENERAL URSINE
(out of the blue)

He speaks the truth! Indeed, we are your brothers!

GENERAL TIGRIS

Inconceivable! Do not tempt to subvert us with your trickery and lies!

(A Tigris soldier drags ZERO forward. He stands nervously, gripping the strap of his guitar case, as GENERAL TIGRIS circles him. He sizes ZERO up, like a tiger hunting its prey)

GENERAL TIGRIS

I've never set eyes on you before. Who are you…? Infiltrator! Speak the truth!

(discovers the guitar case on ZERO's back)

What is this foreign weapon you carry?

ZERO

This is no weapon! It is an instrument!

GENERAL TIGRIS

Everything is a weapon, an instrument of war!

ZERO

Not for war, just a guitar!
It's for singing, for music, for harmony!

GENERAL TIGRIS

Sounds like a load of mumbo jumbo to me. Nothing then to resolve the question of who you are, or where you come from.

(points at ZERO's white T-shirt and jeans)

Where is your armor? This is war! How dare you hail into a battlefield wearing nothing but… undergarments?

ZERO
(offended)

Undergarments? Why, this is what is in vogue, it's the latest fashion!

GENERAL TIGRIS

You make no sense; your time is up!
Will you fight, surrender, or will you lose your head? Answer me!

ZERO

I… I… I refuse!

GENERAL TIGRIS

Refuse to do what? That was not an option!

ZERO

I have no reason to fight. I have no reason to surrender.

GENERAL TIGRIS

There is no need for reason—this is a matter of survival, it is inevitable! We must kill to live! Do I make myself clear?

ZERO

Oh, you're clear, crystal clear. It doesn't change my decision not to fight.

(He pauses in frustration, then comes up with a bright idea)

Wait a minute…

(ZERO stops talking and walks over to the Ursine Army. He goes up to one of the soldiers and strums a chord in the soldier's face. The chord reverberates through the air, filling the silence of the stage until it fades out. The soldier stands still as a statue, without batting an eye. The Ursine Army stands frozen as if somebody has hit the pause button)

ZERO

Just look, look closely! They're just… shadows! Images that don't exist!

GENERAL TIGRIS

It doesn't matter!

SOLDIERS OF TIGRIS ARMY

It doesn't matter! Stab and destroy!
We're in for the kill!

SOLDIERS OF URSINE ARMY
(unfreezing and joining in)

Stab and destroy! We're in for the kill!

GENERAL TIGRIS

Seize this imposter, and tie him up to the pole!

ZERO

I am no imposter!

GENERAL URSINE
(butting in again)

He's right, he is not lying!

(GENERAL URSINE steps forward, rips off his armor, which is made of paper, and says mockingly with a sneer)

Look, we are all just paper. With the words
enemy written on it. Just a name, no,
a concept written on paper.

GENERAL TIGRIS

Nonsense! Just nonsense!
Shut down this scheming nonsense at once!

SONG OF GENERAL TIGRIS

Take it or leave it
When I say war I mean war
Take it or leave it
When I say games I mean games
Brothers are family, foes are enemy
Take it or leave it, I say it, I mean it
So, sound off my men, marching to my drill.

SOLDIERS OF TIGRIS ARMY

Stab and destroy, we're in for the kill!

GENERAL TIGRIS

I see it clearly now! You're a spy from their side!

ZERO

No, you've got it all wrong! I am your descendant, from a time in the future!

GENERAL TIGRIS

Lies! Lies! Lies! Nothing but lies. That is your number one offense! Soldiers! Tie him up.

GENERAL URSINE

Agreed! Squash the lying bug before the real battle!

SOLDIERS FROM BOTH ARMIES

Stab and destroy! We're in for the kill!

(The Tigris Army and Ursine Army put their swords down and together they capture ZERO and tie him to a stake, which stands in the spot of the old tree from Scene 1)

ZERO

(struggles to break free)

I am no spy, believe me! I'm not. This is all a huge misunderstanding! Spare my innocent life, I beg of you!

(The soldiers ignore his pleas. United in purpose, they sing together in harmony)

SONG OF SOLDIERS

We all may burn to ashes, but we don't care
Are we soldiers or are we puppets
Just the same extra lives to spare
We'll set fire and destroy, murder and bloody slay
We cannot be faulted; it's human history in play
War after war… war after war
We've woken from this nightmare
Countless times before.

(The soldiers tighten the rope around ZERO and cover his eyes with a blindfold. Both Generals, satisfied with their soldiers' work, come forward and shake hands)

GENERAL TIGRIS

General Ursine, it seems a common enemy has brought us together for once. Why don't we call a truce and take a well-deserved break, before we head into our next great battle?

GENERAL URSINE

Another thing we can agree on! What a miracle this is.

(chuckles)

Rest up, you'll need your energy, seeing that my men are going to demolish your little army!

GENERAL TIGRIS

(laughs)

Seems like we could use a crazy guy every now and then.

GENERAL URSINE

Who would have guessed? Amid battle, a crazy guy would bring us peace!

(Soldiers bring forward a table with a feast, and the two generals raise their drinking horns. As they are about to cheer each other,

a loud shattering noise is heard, and an eerie silence sweeps over the merriment, pausing all action)

GENERAL TIGRIS
(steps forward)

What now?

GENERAL URSINE
(raising his brow)

What now, what?

GENERAL TIGRIS

What was that?

GENERAL URSINE

What was that noise?

GENERAL TIGRIS
(looking at the drinking horn in his hand)

Perhaps we have toasted with these drinking horns a little too eagerly.

GENERAL URSINE
(looking at the horn in his hand)

Or we have locked horns a little too early.

GENERAL TIGRIS
(chuckles as he disarms)

It seems like we think alike.

GENERAL URSINE
(smiling as he disarms as well)

It seems like we are alike.

(Both Generals bang drinking horns together and down their drinks. The merriment resumes and laughter fills the stage)

GENERAL TIGRIS
(looking into GENERAL URSINE's face)

This may be the alcohol talking, but we even sort of look-alike! Are you real?

GENERAL URSINE

If it's the alcohol talking, what seems real must be real! Wouldn't you agree?

GENERAL TIGRIS
(laughs uncontrollably)

This is too crazy! You're right. We're a spitting image! And to think all this time, we've just been trying to spit at each other!

GENERAL URSINE

We've been too crazy fighting! Let's only do battle… when we're too crazy to fight!

GENERAL TIGRIS
(raising his drinking horn)

To crazy fighting!

(The generals toast each other, down their drinks and toss the horns aside)

SONG OF THE GENERALS

Stab and destroy, we're in for the kill
One road to survival, the moral downhill
There can only be a single sun in the sky
No room to yield, no time for allies
Stab and destroy! The only lesson we've learned
We're in for the kill! The only trust we've earned
We stand as an army, battles lost and won
We stand together, we stand as one.

(War drums beat loudly. ZERO, still tied to the stake, looks up at the sky and sings in outrage)

ZERO'S SONG II

No, no, no... can't stand it anymore
Might as well be the same as before
I left to find peace. I left to belong
Destined for nowhere, but dead and wrong
Ah, ah, ah... death to romance, death to love
No matter where you look, just hatred above
I've travelled through time
With hopes of finding some light
I must leave this darkness
I must leave this fight.

(As he sings the final verse, ZERO's body falls as limp as a bird with broken wings. Everything grows dark around him. A stranger (not SHADOW) stealthily approaches ZERO, checks the coast is clear, and hands him a vessel of wine to quench his thirst. While ZERO drinks the wine, the stranger whispers in his ear)

STRANGER

(in the voice of OLD MAN)

Look, young man. Behind you? That's a cliff! And below that? That's the Han River! Take a leap in that direction! It's your path to survival. It is not a path for the faint of heart. It's a choice given to the brave. Those who risk everything with no fear of death!

(ZERO is surprised when he recognizes STRANGER's voice. Gathering strength he pulls the stake that he is tied to out of the ground. He walks backwards, facing the soldiers. When he is sure no one is looking, he leaps off the cliff)

ZERO

What a nightmare!

(A loud splash is heard. SHADOW nods and exits the stage)

LIGHTS OUT

SCENE 3

(Transported through time again, the year is now 3020. A grand City Hall stands in place of the battlefield and bus stop. What used to be a stake, and then a tree, is now a tall clock tower. It is assembly time for City Hall employees who stand in rows wearing protective gear resembling hazmat suits with astronaut helmets. The sound of a ticking clock grows louder. As the hour hand hits twelve, tower bells peal. ZERO appears on the stage, flopping and flapping like a fish out of water)

(The employees stare blankly. With his messy hair and dishevelled look, ZERO stands out amongst the immaculate rows of employees)

(In the future humanoid robots rule humans and hold all leadership roles)

(Humanoid Robot managers march robotically to the front of the stage and stand in front of the human employees. The assembly begins to sing, without emotion)

SONG OF THE HUMANOID ROBOTS

Machines are artificial, Humanoids are artificial
Love is illegal, Duty is essential
In this complete Utopia, our flawless paradise
The lines are clear, clean-cut, concise
Love is inferior, an overrated distraction
Life comes pre-planned, death is its destination
Life is engineered with a test tube and flask
Death too is engineered with a gas mask.

(As the song nears the end, MAYOR-BOT enters. A humanoid built as an authoritative figure, he is tall in stature, large and overbearing, and wears a tailored suit)

MAYOR-BOT
(with artificial enthusiasm)

Good morning, everybody!

EMPLOYEES

Good morning, Mayor!

(ZERO hastily tries to find a place in line amongst the human employees but sticks out like the proverbial sore thumb. MAYOR-BOT sensing something is different, scans the rows of employees and stops when he discovers ZERO)

MAYOR-BOT

I have detected an abnormality.

(circles around ZERO, scanning him up and down)
This is not regulation attire. Where is your identification? Are you human?

ZERO
(confused)

Do I not look human?

MAYOR-BOT

The heightened emotion levels in your voice may suggest that you are human. Where is your helmet, unidentified human?

ZERO
(looks around at the other human employees, confused)

A helmet?

MAYOR-BOT

The lack of proper attire may suggest that you are a human with a willingness to die. The human lung does not come equipped with a filtration system, thus will reach maximum contamination within approximately sixty to seventy-five minutes of breathing air with the current carbon monoxide levels.

(scans ZERO up and down again)

Does your lack of proper attire suggest (A) you are a human with substandard knowledge, or (B) you are a human

with a superfluous ego? Either way...
(lifts its hand to signal a Humanoid Robot manager)
... we will provide a regulation helmet for you.

ZERO
(in shock)

I knew this day would come eventually!
(starts to cough)
I can't,
(cough)
breathe!

MAYOR-BOT

The unidentified human requires a helmet immediately.

(MAYOR-BOT's secretary, FEMALE, takes a step forward. She takes off her helmet, placing it in ZERO's hands)

FEMALE

Quickly, put it on and activate the filtration system.

MAYOR-BOT

Your comradeship with fellow mankind is appreciated. Your willingness to sacrifice your life for others suggests feminine empathy and maternal instinct. This data point will be noted in the next Life Manufacturing evaluation—perhaps we will increase the number of female embryos to increase our empathy statistics in future generations. Of course, we will have to weigh up the negative effects of increased female population in the human mix.

ZERO

Thank… you…

(breathing rapidly)

I feel like…

(coughing)

I'm about to suffocate!

(FEMALE takes the helmet from ZERO's hands and places it firmly on his head. She presses a button on the side, activating the filtration system. ZERO's coughing slows down, and he takes a deep breath. He finally looks at FEMALE and gazes into her eyes. Suddenly, an alarm bell sounds. MAYOR-BOT interprets it as an alarm to wrap up the assembly, but it is an alarm detecting heightened love interest in the vicinity)

(SHADOW enters backstage, stands in the corner, a bystander observing the scene)

MAYOR-BOT

(speaks in an artificially enthused tone)

That will be the end of our assembly! Everyone is to return to their workstations immediately.

EMPLOYEES

Yes, Mayor!

MAYOR-BOT

The next break will be in eighty-seven minutes and forty seconds.

EMPLOYEES

Yes, Mayor!

MAYOR-BOT

Your full concentration is required. Unnecessary social interactions, including non-work-related conversation and physical contact, are strictly forbidden.

EMPLOYEES

Yes, Mayor!

(The human employees march out of the square in line formation, leaving ZERO behind. He looks around, unsure of where to go)

MAYOR-BOT

Unidentified Human, it appears you are still here. You are required to be at your workstation for another eighty-five minutes and twenty seconds. Your earlier actions suggest there may be an error in your genome.

(MAYOR-BOT lifts his hand, signaling to FEMALE to step forward. She receives a new helmet from a Humanoid Robot manager and puts it on her head. She steps forward next to MAYOR-BOT)

You are to take this unidentified human to the hospital immediately, to receive a full genome scan, including inherent faults and environmental errors.

(ZERO, confused, attempts to ask a question. FEMALE quickly intervenes, blocking him from MAYOR-BOT's line of vision)

FEMALE

Yes, Mayor.

MAYOR-BOT

Proceed as instructed.

FEMALE

Yes, Mayor.

ZERO

(still unsure of what's happening)

Hospital? What hospital?
I'm not a fan of needles!

FEMALE

(in a hushed voice)

Just be quiet, keep it down and follow me.

(MAYOR-BOT exits. ZERO and FEMALE stand in the dark hallway on the side)

ZERO

(shifting his helmet around)

Do I need to keep this bulky thing on?

FEMALE

Always. Can a fish live out of water?
If you'd like to find out, you can take it off.

(pauses)

Keep it on. It is necessary for survival.

ZERO

(sarcastically)

What a place to live!

FEMALE

(raises a brow)

You're... different. Where are you from?

ZERO

Erm… that is… well… funny story.

FEMALE

Oh, are you part of that space exploration project, the one where they send faulty-genome humans?

ZERO

(offended)

Um, no?

(clears his throat)

I am from…

FEMALE

I read that there have been a couple of instances like this recently.

(nervously paces back and forth)

That makes you… a liability.
If the mayor finds out…

ZERO

The mayor? That robot in charge?

(checks FEMALE to see if he's right)

I'm right, aren't I? It's a robot, right? Ha! Will you look at that? We always joked about the robot lords taking over, but for it to be a reality! Unbelievable!

FEMALE

I don't see what's so unbelievable about it. The robots are superior across all fronts. They have advanced society to new heights in a fraction of the time that it would have taken us humans. There is no irrational error, no inequity, no decision made without reason. There are no politicians or fraudsters. Their knowledge is light years ahead of us, their calculations are always correct. They do not make mistakes, and they always have an answer. The only problem we have in our society today is humans wanting more freedom than what they have been allotted. Otherwise, life is pretty damn perfect. That's if you don't fall in love.

ZERO

No love? What could be more important to the human soul? And no freedom!

FEMALE

Quiet, before someone hears us.
Let's get out of here before you say anything else.

ZERO

Where to?

FEMALE

Just follow me.

(ZERO and FEMALE exit stage left. SHADOW shrugs and follows)

LIGHTS OUT

SCENE 4

(ZERO and FEMALE enter her apartment. Everything in the futuristic apartment is neatly arranged in modular cubes. As they walk in, the full moon rises in the background. It shines upon the apartment, creating an illusion that the two are on the moon)

FEMALE

Well, this is me.

(FEMALE closes the door behind her)

You may speak freely now.

ZERO

(looks around)

Wow, this is more than I expected. Almost like... we're on the moon. Clean, too.

(ZERO runs his fingertips on the table surface)

Too clean, perhaps. How do you live here?

This place is practically empty.
Are you one of those minimalists?

FEMALE
(shrugs)

What more do I need?
The state takes care of everything.

ZERO

Surely, they can't take care of everything.
How do you spend your downtime?
Do you listen to music? Read books?

FEMALE

Books? What are those?

ZERO
(gasps with horror)

What are... books? You've never seen a book before?

(mumbles to himself)

Just a pretty face, I see.

(clears throat)

Ahem, books are rectangular objects made by the art of binding paper together. You can hold a book in your hand. Cover to cover, very simple, on the outside. Yet, when you open the cover and read that first page, they transform into doors! The words that we speak are written with ink on each page. The written word is the key to unlocking new worlds, a free ticket to enter new universes!

All you need are your eyes, and your ability to read, to have years and decades of new experiences. Music is great, it brings light to the darkest days, but books! Books are vital to the essence of human life!

FEMALE

Oh, I think I know what you're talking about. Books! That... archaic data storage system that took up physical space, I remember hearing about it. The carbon footprint was too high. Those dinosaurs of print are extinct. A great relief for mankind!

ZERO

(mortified)

Did you say relief? No, no, it's an absolute horror, a disgrace! Cleaning up house is one thing but bleaching away everything, including things that nurture us in our daily lives? Unacceptable. I can't stay here anymore. I need a way out! Oh, where are my manners? I forgot to thank you... for saving my life.

FEMALE
(blushing)

Don't mention it.

ZERO

No really, you saved me. Without you, I would've suffocated.

FEMALE

You reminded me of someone.

ZERO

Quite the pick-up line.

FEMALE
(doesn't hear him)

My little brother. He was tested for faulty genomes. They sent him… to disposal.

ZERO
(stands back with surprise)

Disposal?
For what?

FEMALE
(sadly)

What else would it be?

ZERO

What was he part of a rebellion?

FEMALE

You could call it that. He was in favor of Traditionalism and voiced his opinion about bringing back the old cabinet. He was ostracized from his organization and put on trial. He was sent to the chambers in the hospital, a few years ago, right around this time. Once you're sentenced to disposal… there's no turning back.

ZERO

Atrocious!

FEMALE

An atrocity indeed.

ZERO

I guess even a perfect world has its rebels. You remind me of somebody too, you know.

FEMALE

I do?

(ZERO and FEMALE lock eyes with each other, and everything stops. The lighting in the apartment slowly changes colors. Music fades into the background)

FEMALE

I've never... felt anything like this before. It's like somebody put a buzzer right... here.

(points to her chest)

It's buzzing, no palpitating, with urgency... with something!

(flustered)

I'm supposed to report to the authorities immediately if I... feel... anything like this. Then I'll have to be examined... and receive treatment... but... I don't want to!

ZERO

Report to whom?

FEMALE

The authorities.

ZERO
(confused)

For what?

FEMALE

Feelings... like this... like... love.
It's forbidden between male and female.
It's illegal.

ZERO
(shocked)

And the atrocity continues! Why would that be outlawed? For what reason?

FEMALE

It's a waste of human resources.

ZERO

Well, if there's no love, how are babies made now? Hmm?

FEMALE

Oh please, it's been more than two hundred years since humans have been bred by artificial insemination and incubation. I was born in the lab. We have all been born in the lab.

ZERO

You don't say!

FEMALE
(proudly)

It's true! There is no room for error with the advanced birthing system. No room for flawed DNA, only the best genes are combined to create the absolute best—designer babies if you will. Of course, humans will never rule, but still…

ZERO

(grimacing)

It sounds terrible! What a future to look forward to...

FEMALE

(shakes her head vigorously)

You've got it all wrong—don't think of it like that! Our society is ruled by reason and efficiency, thanks to artificial intelligence. Much better than where we were a thousand years ago, don't you think? There are no wars, no bloodbaths. It's substantial progress!

ZERO

Progress, progress! All this talk of progress…

(switching his tone)

makes me want to progress our relationship one step, no, one kiss further.

FEMALE

(shyly)

Well, we'd need to take these helmets off for that to happen. And even after that, we won't have that much time before we stop breathing in this air, so we need to get it over with quickly.

ZERO

Get it over with?

(sarcastically)

How romantic!

FEMALE

What? It's efficient!

ZERO

In what world do love and efficiency go hand in hand?

FEMALE

In this world! Efficiency is the ultimate paradigm.

(ZERO takes off his helmet and throws it down, walking towards FEMALE. She holds her arms out and stops him in his tracks)

FEMALE

Not so fast!

ZERO

We don't have much time left, so I need to spend every second kissing you!

FEMALE

Seriously, we need to wait. Long story short, I have yet to build immunity to your saliva.

These helmets caused our immune systems to become vulnerable to any type of bacteria. I heard that people from the past were found with all sorts of viruses and bacteria in their bloodstream. Who knows what you could be carrying?

ZERO
(sighs)

Is this what romance looks like in the future?

FEMALE

I've told you already. Love is illegal!

(FEMALE picks up her bag from the corner and pulls out a syringe. She injects medication into her upper arm, as if she were diabetic, then puts the syringe away and takes her helmet off. FEMALE and ZERO share a brief, yet tender kiss. Suddenly, alarm bells blare. FEMALE jumps back in surprise)

ZERO
(unphased)

Calm down. Am I making you nervous?
I don't mean to. I just want to be close to you.

FEMALE
(pushes ZERO away)

Shh! Someone is coming!

(As FEMALE and ZERO put their helmets back on, a loud banging is heard at the door)

POLICE-BOT

Police! Open up!

FEMALE

(panicking)

W-w-what? W-wait… Ju-just a minute!

(FEMALE tries to calm herself for a second, takes a deep breath and opens the door. POLICE-BOT, an intimidatingly tall robot, stands in the doorway, then strides into the apartment. Behind it follows SHADOW. SHADOW closes the door and stands in the corner)

POLICE-BOT

You're under arrest!

ZERO

For what?

POLICE-BOT

An unusual amount of romantic energy has been detected in this location.

ZERO

An unusual amount of what? And how would you know that?

POLICE-BOT

The building detector picked it up.

ZERO

A detector? Like a smoke detector?

POLICE-BOT

The two are similar in concept.

ZERO

Look, all we did was kiss, nothing more. And we're getting arrested? That's blowning it out of proportion; don't you think?

POLICE-BOT

It is not my decision. It is the rules. The detector reported romantic energy units exceeding the legally permissible limit, traceable to this apartment.

ZERO

This is crazy! Where's your warrant?

FEMALE

(pulling ZERO back)

You must know that in our era, warrants are an outdated concept. Our society is built upon a flawless trust system, as there is no dishonesty. Unlike your world in the past, there is no misrepresentation, inequality, or deception.

ZERO

I still have rights, don't I? Go ahead, read me my rights!

(POLICE-BOT immediately responds to ZERO's demands with indifference. It is not offended, and it does not display any emotion towards forcefulness or violence. It is simply answering a question. It is calm and collected. POLICE-BOT pulls out a screen with the constitution listed and scrolls to the relevant chapter)

POLICE-BOT

According to the constitution manual Chapter XII, any physical contact or sexual conduct between members of the opposite sex is deemed unimportant and unnecessary. However, if such actions are taken because of, or are accompanied by, heightened emotional energy of romantic love, it is detrimental to society and must be discontinued before risking further contagion. It is classified as a High Priority offence.

ZERO

What a farce this, advanced society, turned out to be! It goes against instinct, common sense, and human nature! You are all cowards, nothing but complete and absolute cowards!

FEMALE

Please, don't insult us. We are more advanced than you could ever imagine.

ZERO

Advanced, perhaps, but in a doubtful direction.

POLICE-BOT

You are both under arrest.

ZERO

For what crime?

POLICE-BOT

For committing the act of romance.

ZERO

(puts his wrists out in disgust)

If that's the truth, then cuff me, officer.

(POLICE-BOT handcuffs ZERO and FEMALE, then escorts them off the stage. SHADOW follows them with a worried expression. The clock ticks loudly, filling the void of the empty apartment)

LIGHTS OUT

SCENE 5

(The hospital courtroom lights up with a bright cold fluorescent glow. The room is spotless and white, with a visual frigidity creating the illusion that the room is inside a glacier. DOCTOR-BOT sits in the middle of the Judge's bench, wearing a white doctor's gown and glasses with thick rims but no lenses. POLICE-BOT strides in, followed by FEMALE and ZERO. The two humans move as if they are frozen fish strung on a rope. SHADOW quietly follows the group. Everybody takes their places in court, SHADOW finds a seat in the corner and sits down)

POLICE-BOT

Your honor, I present to you the accused.
Please proceed with your judgment.

DOCTOR-BOT

Your service is appreciated.

ZERO
(confused)

I thought we were going to the police station. Isn't this a hospital?

FEMALE

It is. This is where everything happens: life, death, and disposal. Were things different in your time?

ZERO

Sure… in a way, I suppose. But, for trial? For punishment?

FEMALE

Streamlined for efficiency.

POLICE-BOT
(saluting DOCTOR-BOT)

Good day, sir.

DOCTOR-BOT

Indeed, good day.

(DOCTOR-BOT turns its icy chair towards the screen showing the court files. As he scans it, text scrolls at lightning speed)

DOCTOR-BOT

It appears that we have a criminal case to evaluate, not a surgical case.

ZERO

(mockingly whispers to FEMALE)

It appears this one is a judge, not a doctor.

(SHADOW nods from the corner)

FEMALE

Shh, respect for the court, please.

(SHADOW holds his index finger to his lips in agreement. ZERO ignores this and glares at DOCTOR-BOT with blatant defiance. DOCTOR-BOT, finished with its scanning, looks at ZERO and pauses, blankly staring into ZERO's defiant eyes as if it is trying to process what is happening. After a prolonged staring session, DOCTOR-BOT finishes its evaluation and proceeds to speak)

DOCTOR

It appears that in this case, a dangerous condition we thought to be eradicated, stands before us. A genome scan is unnecessary, and as there is a high risk of contagion, the case will be escalated in a time-sensitive nature.

ZERO

You're kidding me!

DOCTOR-BOT

Such remarks could lead to being held in contempt of court.

ZERO

For what? What have I done?

DOCTOR-BOT

Your eyes are emitting dangerous levels of defiance.

ZERO

What? Since when is it illegal to stare at someone?

DOCTOR-BOT

Defiant energy is considered fatally destructive. It leads to treason against the system and can be highly contagious. Early detection and rapid response are the most effective methods of prevention.

ZERO

Ridiculous! I don't get a say in what I say, what I feel, or what I see. When did free will become outlawed?

DOCTOR-BOT

Free will is the ultimate weakness of the human species. It is the precise reason why artificial intelligence will always be superior to humans. We shall not waste any more time with frivolous discussions regarding a crime of passion committed by a substandard being.

ZERO

What you're saying is… I definitely don't have a say in this!

DOCTOR-BOT

(reciting robotically)

The verdicts are now in correct order. This is hospital court, State versus unidentified human male, case number one, count A, romance of the first degree. The defendant is found guilty of the crime of romance, reaching levels detrimental to society. Count B, contempt of court. The defendant is found guilty of contempt, as he not only fails to display any recognition or remorse towards his crimes of count A, but also demonstrated verbal and physical contempt towards the established criminal justice system. This court finds the defendant guilty, and he is to be sentenced to immediate disposal. Case number two, State versus human female, identification number 085B1. While the defendant is found guilty of the crime of romance, she has a strong character history through her years of dedication working at City Hall and recognizes her wrongdoings. She is to be sentenced to a demotion in status and will be reassigned to work in the Labor Department of the Basement. Due to the infectious nature of the crime of romance, this court declares this case a time-sensitive threat to society and escalates the formal sentencing to be carried out immediately. Court is adjourned.

(DOCTOR-BOT bangs its icy gavel on the table loudly. SHADOW, shocked, collapses to the floor)

(The room is instantly transformed from a courtroom to an operating theatre. The door opens and four surgical robots glide in. Without asking permission, two of them examine ZERO and FEMALE, taking blood pressure, drawing blood, and checking their ears and eyes. The other robots wheel in a giant medical device and install it in the center of the room. Once they are ready, they scrub up and prepare for surgery. They each grab a surgical tool: a scalpel, a bone saw, a syringe, a large needle, and surgical thread. Holding up their instruments ready for action, they sing in unison)

SONG OF THE MEDICAL ROBOTS

Surrender to the scalpel
It's human fate
A flash and slash
Then you're out the gate
We'll cut, drill, pry
Till you breathe your last breath
Kneel and obey
Through life and till death
We're your grim reapers
North, East, South, West.

ZERO

Is this it? Is this how I die?
Without a chance to ever see you again?

FEMALE

Don't be afraid. With the BXAX shot you may lose consciousness, but it won't be the end for you. I hear they just send you to another world.

ZERO

Another what?

FEMALE

(points to the large device in the middle of the room)

You see that thing, over there? It transports unconscious bodies. It faxes you to another world. No one knows where. All I know is that you will exist, somewhere, someplace. I may be there, I may not. If fate decides in our favor, we may both exist in the same place. But for now, we can't be certain of anything.

ZERO

(confused and emotional, raises his voice)

Oh, I don't understand, no, I just can't.
I just want to be with you, everywhere, all the time.

FEMALE

That's not possible. You are from the past era, from an… unevolved species of man. You need to go through the due purification process. That might increase the likelihood of our paths crossing at another time.

ZERO

How could you be so calm, so… logical? I can't even see what's in front of me through this torrent of tears!

SONG OF THE LOVERS

(ZERO)

I beg you, my love, don't leave me behind
Alone in the darkness, I'm deaf, I'm blind
Hold me forever in your soft moonlight
Guide me, be with me day and night.

(FEMALE)

Listen, my love, it's a dying shame
Our time is too short, with no one to blame
Yet we've got our memories
Our tale of true love
The dream to dream forever
Our lasting mourning dove.

(DUET)

Come closer, my love, come near
At any moment, all we know may disappear
One last kiss, one last embrace
This memory is forever, in this time, this space.

(The facsimile machine whirs up, overriding the sound of their singing. The surgical robots grab ZERO by his limbs and attempt to shove him into the machine opening. ZERO fights back, screaming and kicking. SHADOW anxiously watches from the corner, pulling at his hair and pacing back and forth)

ZERO

This can't be it!
My life can't be ended by the hands of…
robots!

FEMALE
(panicks as the reality settles in)

No! Please, please, stop!

(ZERO tries to escape the machine, pressing all the buttons on the machine, but it accelerates pulling ZERO further in. As ZERO cries out in agony, FEMALE jumps in, pushing ZERO out of the way and taking his place. She disappears into the machine, ZERO tumbles onto the ground and loses consciousness)

(Music by Max Richter, 'A Lamenting Song', plays in the background)

(As the music comes to an end, the machine's status changes from a red 'In Process' to a green 'Complete'. ZERO slowly gains consciousness, pulling himself up. He looks around. When he realizes FEMALE has disappeared, he breaks down sobbing. He yanks the power cord to disconnect the machine and tries to break

it with various instruments lying around the room. He attacks the machine, then hurls himself at the surgical robots, ripping their limbs off like a tiger. Electrical sparks fly from the fuse box and the machine catches fire. The room becomes a chaotic mess. Sparks fly from all corners, smoke fills the once icy-white clean room)

(ZERO, exhausted, coughs from the smoke and collapses to the floor. SHADOW gravely walks towards him and embraces his limp body. He picks ZERO up onto his shoulders, and lugs him out of the chaos, saving ZERO from his worst nightmare. They exit offstage)

(With a loud electrical buzz, all lights shut off. The fire dies down with the blaring of the smoke alarm and the whoosh of sprinklers in the background. As the noise of the sprinklers fades, a loud splash is heard in the distance… somebody has jumped into the deep waters of the Han River)

LIGHTS OUT

SCENE 6

(The sun begins to set, back at the bus stop by the Han River. The set is the same as SCENE 1, except there is now a broken bicycle leaning against the old tree)

(ZERO is asleep at the bus stop, using his guitar case as a pillow. BOY enters from behind the tree, tossing a rubber ball around as he sings)

BOY'S SONG

Round and around, around goes the ball
Take a wrong turn and oops! Down you fall
Round and around, let it roll and run
Life is just a dream dreamt under the sun
Kick the ball as high as you can
It spins right back to where you stand
You can run, you can hide
Just a dream, that's all
Round and around and around goes the ball.

(BOY sings as he tosses the ball in the air as if he were a circus juggler. The song comes to an end, as he misses the ball. It rolls away towards ZERO, nudging him awake)

ZERO
(sits up suddenly)

Where is this?
Where am I?
Which world am I in?
Where have I been?

(ZERO paces frantically, shouting and gesturing towards thin air. BOY cautiously grabs his ball and runs out of sight, hiding behind the tree)

ZERO
(looking around)

Who's there?
I thought I heard singing!
Is anybody there?
(shaking his head)
What time is it? Seems like the sun is about to set... So...?

(ZERO continues mumbling to himself)

ZERO

Hell... What a nightmare that was! Wait, what is this?

(ZERO realizes he carries a helmet in his right hand and holds a ticket stub in his left. He shrieks, jumping back in shock)

ZERO

What the…! What are these?

(ZERO throws the helmet and ticket stub down and scratches his head trying to remember. He scratches harder, then starts pulling out his hair like a crazed man. BOY runs out from his hiding place, attempting to stop him)

BOY

Mister, sir, please! Are you okay?

ZERO

(continuing to pull at his hair)

A helmet! Oh… oooh… and tickets? Who's going to believe me? Who in their right mind would believe that reality… is multi-layered? Who would know that? All I know is that they're going to point their fingers and lock me up with the loonies!

BOY

Um… mister? What are you mumbling about?

ZERO

(finally notices BOY)

Who are you?

BOY

I ask you the same, mister. Who are you?

ZERO

I guess I have no idea who I even am right now. Everything is jumbled and muddled!

BOY

Oh boy… the hospital is a long way from here.

ZERO

Hey kid, do me a favor, tell me the date?

BOY

Today?

ZERO

You heard me.

BOY

(confused)

The date? All I know is that today is… today.

ZERO

Sure, sure, that's not wrong. That's right… all we have is today. Time could be like that… without clear boundaries, like water flowing in the Han River.

BOY

Speaking of flowing… Why are you sweating so much?

(takes a step closer)

Your clothes are drenched! And…

(sniffs)

you stink!

ZERO

I went for a swim in the Han River.

BOY

You're kidding me.

ZERO

It's true. I went for a long… long swim.

BOY

You know, grown-ups like you should set better examples for kids like me. You better watch what you say. Besides, I saw you taking a nap under that tree!

ZERO

Oh, I see, you only believe what you can see. One day you'll learn that there is a reality in the unseeable. Like love. True love. I experienced that.

BOY

Must've been a nice dream.

ZERO

Yeah... well, life is all a dream anyway, so you could say that.

(ZERO walks up to the tree and starts to sing, leaning with a glazed expression)

ZERO'S SONG III

I may have lost love, but not the memories
She left me alone, alone to burn and freeze
A turbulent place for a lonely vagabond
I cannot stay
I must move forward and beyond
Our time was short, fleeting, now gone
But I'll carry the beauty of our love
Forever on.

(ZERO strokes the trunk of the tree. He reaches down and dips his hand in the muddy puddle, creating a ripple. He checks this is the spot where it all began)

(Overwhelmed with emotion, he reminds himself he is not alone, and holds back tears, looking towards the distance and into the pink and orange-hued skies of the sunset)

ZERO

Look at that sun, off towards the West
to shine upon another world. Hey kid, did
you happen to see an old man around? He's
supposed to meet me here at sunset.

BOY

An old man?

ZERO

Yeah, a very old man. He's short, about your height, just a bag of bones with dark spots all over like a fossil.

BOY

I haven't seen anybody like that. I've been here all day, since early morning mister, and I haven't seen any old man around.

ZERO

You haven't? You swear you've been here since morning?

BOY

I'm not lying.

ZERO

Hmph.

(talking to himself)

Odd. So odd. So, there was no old man to begin with. As if… it never happened. As if… I've been… dreaming. Then what's this? What are these, that I find in my hands? What did I find in my right hand? And my left hand? Baffling, bewildering, such a disconcerting mishmash!

(pauses, then turns to BOY)

Then again, you kid, what are you doing here? What have you been doing here, from dawn to dusk?

(BOY points at the broken bicycle. The bicycle looks worn out, barely leaning against the tree)

BOY

My bike is broken. I'm waiting for someone.

ZERO

For someone?

BOY

Someone who can fix my wheels.

ZERO

Wheel? Who would that be?

BOY

I have no idea.

ZERO

What a strange thing to say, kid.
How old are you, by the way?

BOY

A hundred!

(laughs)

Just kidding. Take out a zero, and that's my age! I'm ten.

ZERO

Good to know. What's your name?

BOY

Bring back the zero, and that's my name!
I'm Zero.

ZERO

What? No way! Impossi-…wait, what?

(A young woman, resembling FEMALE enters the scene. She hurries past the bus stop, holding up a black umbrella. ZERO looks at her in surprise)

ZERO

Excuse me… miss? Hello?
Could you please, wait a moment?

(runs after the woman)

Please stop! I must ask you something!

(The woman hurries off the stage, without turning back. ZERO follows her, exiting off stage. BOY walks slowly, his hands clasped behind his back in an elderly manner. As ZERO runs out, BOY speaks in the voice of OLD MAN)

BOY

(in OLD MAN's voice)

Tsk, tsk. Oh, to still be so blind!
After everything he's seen! Perhaps he needed to see more. To see what or who is in front of him! Useless. Completely useless.

(clears his throat, coughing like an old man)

And yet, what is the point of life, if we can't experience a little magic now and then? Ah yes, yes, of course. That's all there is to it, of course.

(BOY turns around, picking his ball up from the ground. He kicks it around, bouncing it up and down as he sings the finale song)

BOY'S SONG II

Round and around and around goes the ball
Take a big spin and oomph! Down you fall
Round and around, you may slip and swoon
Life is just a dream dreamt under the moon
You can reach, jump up, drop down and roll
We're all spinning circles in a fishbowl
Are we here, are we there, have we hit a wall
Who knows, but hey! Around goes the ball.

LIGHTS OUT & CURTAIN

SUE JA JOO

Sue Ja Joo is a highly acclaimed playwright, novelist, poet, and visual artist. The plays in *'Zero'* have been performed onstage at Dream Theatre in Seoul, Korea, since 2017.

Sue Ja Joo was born in Seoul, Korea. She emigrated in 1976, living abroad for 23 years in France, Switzerland, and the United States. She returned to Korea in 1998. Holding a B.A. in Fine Arts (Seoul National University) and an M.A. degree from Colgate Rochester Crozer Divinity School, Sue's literary inspiration comes from her deep roots in aesthetics, religion, and global cultures.

In 2013, she became the first recipient of the Insung Park Mini-Fiction Literary Award, which recognizes her achievements in popularizing this genre in Korea. She is at the frontier of a new literary genre, 'Smart Fiction' which hybridizes poetry and short fiction.

Sue is currently working as the editor-in-chief of a literary magazine based in Seoul. Sue Ja Joo resides in South Korea.

www.ingramcontent.com/pod-product-compliance
Lightning Source LLC
Chambersburg PA
CBHW040514170726
48295CB00012B/190